Home Life

A History:

The United Methodist Children's Home
of the
North Georgia Conference

By
William Gerald Winkler

ISBN: 1-890307-38-6

Boyd Publishing Company
PO Box 367
Milledgeville, Georgia 31061

TABLE OF CONTENTS

The Reverend Jesse M. Boring, 1807-1890.
Founder of the United Methodist Children's Home in
Decatur, Georgia

i. Preface

This history of the North Georgia Conference's United Methodist Children's Home in Decatur, Georgia began with a few simple questions to Mr. Beverly Cochran, the administrator of the UMC Home. My wife Elaine and I had worked as auxiliary volunteers at the Home for several years preparing for and participating in the semi-annual flea market and bake sales which help raise money for the Home. The longer we worked the more my interest was piqued about the origins of the Home with its spacious campus, its dedicated staff, and its *raison d'etre,* the children. When, where, and why was it established, why was it located at 500 Columbia Drive in Decatur, and a hundred other questions would surface as we worked, all wanting an answer.

As a retired epidemiologist I had been trained to ask questions, to sift through the answers, and to arrive at logical, hopefully correct answers. I began to inquire of all the people at the Home with whom I worked, where and why was this place? Unfortunately, none of my fellow workers had any answers and none of them seemed overly interested in learning why or wherefore the place existed. Clearly it would be necessary to pursue this at a higher level - hence the approach to Administrator Cochran.

Bev (as Mr. Cochran is familiarly known) was able and willing to answer my questions about the Home and its origins in some detail. After an hour of questions and answers, as I stood and prepared to leave, my curiosity salved, Cochran cleared his throat and admonished me to "hold up a minute". In his most disarming manner he went on to explain that it had been over 50 years since anyone had compiled a history of the Home and a more current one was needed, and why shouldn't I do this as I obviously was interested in such things. Flattered and caught completely by surprise, I demurred briefly and then agreed to have a go at it. Some time later I confronted Cochran and allowed that had I realized the enormity of the task I would never have consented to take it on. His response was "Yes, I know, that's why I didn't tell you. If I had, you would likely never have agreed to do it." He was probably correct.

Over the subsequent months of seeking out data, interviewing people, reviewing trustees annual reports, student theses, and newspaper accounts etc. I have learned much about the Home and its past, and I have thoroughly enjoyed the exercise. I have used the annual reports of the Trustees of the North Georgia Conference as the framework around which to develop the history. Using those reports as a skeleton I have tried to flesh out details from other sources.

Without doubt the most telling, and from my point of view, by far the most interesting data are those contributed by former residents and staff persons (Chapters 9 and 10). They are, after all, what the Home is all about. Their comments give life to an otherwise very ordinary and uninspiring text.

Unfortunately, most of the comments are from persons who were at the Home during a relatively narrow span of time, 1940 to 1955. These children had been placed in the Home usually because they truly were orphans or because they were from families that were in such financial straits that they could not afford to raise the children. Those who had been in residence prior to the 1940s are fast passing away or are too difficult to interview. For those children institutionalized in the 40s and 50s the Home had become HOME. In so doing it generated an intense affection and loyalty for this place of refuge that they so badly needed, a loyalty and devotion that persists today in former residents even fifty years after they had left the Home. Those who came in the 1960s or later, represent a totally different population with very different backgrounds. Today's residents often are placed in the Home to remove them from dysfunctional family situations rather than because they are orphaned. As such they may suffer from greater psychological and emotional problems than the orphaned children of earlier years. Also, because today's children are outplaced as rapidly as possible, either back to their own families or to foster families, they do not have the time in residence to develop the degree of affection that yesterday's children had for the Home. For example, in the Home's early years children were accepted as early as infancy and generally stayed at the Home until early adulthood, perhaps 12 years on average; by 1978 the average residency period had been reduced to 4 1/2 years; and by 1998 it had been reduced to 9 1/2 months.

Clearly, the attitude of children from the 1940-'50s era concerning the Home may differ from the attitude of children from the '60s and later. Whatever bias this time-selected group of interviewees from the '40s and '50s may introduce is unavoidable and hopefully not too misleading.

My only regret in putting together this history of the Home is that I am not sufficiently skilled as a writer to do justice to the subject. Also, the narrative would clearly have had more meaning if it had been done by a former resident rather than an outsider "looking in." I hope I may be forgiven for errors of commission and omission which clearly had to occur, and I hope this history, however flawed it may be, will help others to appreciate the Home and all those persons past, present, and future who are associated with it.

ii Acknowledgements

Having committed to write a history about a subject with which I had only a superficial acquaintance it became clear early on that I would have to rely heavily on the knowledge and experience of others. And so it has been. While many have contributed to this history and I thank them all, a number of persons have given so much that I must single them out for especial thanks.

First and foremost is Katha Morgan. Her official title is Associate Director for Public Relations, but in fact she is also the unofficial historian for the UMCH, the major bridge (ombudsman) between the UMCH staff and the alumnae, and in her resides much of the institutional memory of the UMCH. Without her freely contributing from her memory and files for this study this history probably could not have been written. Second in importance (arguably could be first) is Administrator Beverly Cochran. Without his initial stimulation and subsequent help this history would never have been started. Thanks to other staff members, especially those who contributed to the Cochran Chapter and to those Home alumnae who contributed recollections for the chapter of that name. They provided much of the substance for this history. I am especially indebted to Julie Spinks Mote, James Burch, and Brenda Bailey Reinhart for their recollections and pictures of life at the Home, and their encouragement when at times the writing seemed an insurmountable task. Special thanks also to Hugh Boring who provided a copy of his compiled history of the Boring family, and to William McKenzie whose personal experience with Home life in a different but similar institution and whose subsequent studies and publications on present and future issues provided a more complete understanding of institutional life and current thinking about its future. Special thanks also to Bill Bozarth whose expertise with computers has been so helpful in developing this document.

Finally, especially heartfelt thanks to my wife Elaine whose understanding, tolerance and encouragement through two years of my preoccupation with this task made it all possible.

Origins of Children's Homes and Orphanages

C hild care facilities (orphanages and children's homes) in the western world emerged as significant social institutions largely as a result of the Industrial Revolution (ca 1750 – 1900). Prior to the 1700s, orphaned, abandoned or otherwise dependent children (and adults) were usually absorbed into the extended family by those most able to provide for them. With agriculture as the main business of society, children worked in the fields alongside adults as their age and abilities permitted. Small children might do light work, such as carrying food pails to field workers or cleaning soil from root crops. Older children worked the fields alongside adults.

Uncared for urban children often were placed by government officials in almshouses (poor houses) where they were crowded in with adult drunks, the mentally disturbed, debtors, and other less desirable persons - a poor environment for young children in need of moral and financial support.

When the Industrial Revolution changed the work force from a primarily agricultural one to an industrial factory based force, the needs and opportunities for work participation changed, as did the potential for worker abuse. In the earliest industrial plants, cotton and woolen mills, and coalmines, children were quickly recognized as a cheap but usable work force. With little recourse, they were badly exploited by uncaring employers concerned primarily with making money for the plant owners and themselves. Many children were little more than slaves; in some cases they were worse off since slaves had monetary value and were worth saving whereas child laborers had little or no intrinsic value to employers and could be easily replaced. Accidents and work related diseases, especially bysinnosis (in cotton mills) and anthracosis (in coal mines) were common, more so among children than adults because of the former's greater susceptibility to disease and their closer physical proximity to factory pollutants than larger adults. Life spans of "factory children" were noticeably shorter than those of their agricultural contemporaries.

Our British forebears sometimes employed less than admirable tactics to cope with the orphan problem. Not uncommonly, the government would "round up" orphans and cause them to be forcibly apprenticed to tradesmen, or worse, send them to the New World as indentured servants. The period of indenture varied from 3 to 10 or more years, but was usually about seven years.

It was in this setting that the great English author, Charles Dickens grew up, and indeed, he suffered many of the abuses and indignities of contemporary orphans though he was not one himself. Born near Portsea, England in 1812, son of a ne'er-do-well father who was sent to debtor's prison when young Dickens was eleven, the author to be would never forget the deprivation and humiliation he suffered as a young child growing up in near poverty. During his father's imprisonment, Dickens was forced to leave school and work in a lampblack factory where he pasted labels on jars. When his father was freed three years later and the family in better financial state, Dickens was able to return to school to complete his education but he never forgot the injustices of his poverty days and this became a major topic in his writings in later years, *viz.* the Bob Crachit family in *Christmas Carol* and the trials and tribulations of the title characters in *David Copperfield* and *Oliver Twist*. As one of the most popular writers in the contemporary English-speaking world, Dickens was influential in sensitizing the British public and government to the societal abuses of the poor, especially the children, which had developed with the Industrial Revolution.

Interestingly, the cry for social reform was coming from another, very different, writer at the same time. Karl Marx, the socialist, also was preaching and writing on the evils and abuses inflicted by factory owners and managers on the impoverished workers of the day. Marx was more vehement in his condemnation of government and industrialists and was less concerned with child abuse than Dickens, but like Dickens, his preachings expressed anger and frustration at the abuse of working people. His calls for open revolution in the name of social reform, especially the publication of his *Communist Manifesto* (coauthored with Friedrich Engels) in January 1848, which proposed sweeping social changes, resulted in his expulsion from several European countries and his eventual settling in London, Dickens hometown. This occurred during the same period as Dickens was at his most influential in writing. Though the two reformers may never have met, their combined influence clearly had impact on the thinking of contemporary Britons and was a factor in the emerging social revolution of the late 19th and early 20th Century.

The movement for reform of exploitative labor practices was not confined to Great Britain or Western Europe. In the United States social consciences were similarly being awakened. Not as heavily industrialized as Western Europe or Britain, in the 1860s the U.S. had another more pressing problem. The American Civil War (1861-1865) had created a huge population of orphans, homeless persons, and others who had been separated from their families during the war.

Children's Homes in the New World

The first orphanage in the New World was a home for girls established in Mexico City by a Catholic Order in 1548. It was called La Caridad and its subsequent status has been lost.

3

In the English speaking New World, even before the societal disruption created by the Civil War, orphanages had been established. The lives of early settlers were fraught with danger - starvation, Indian wars, and disease - to name a few, all contributed to the development of an unusually large orphan population in the colonies. Thus it was that orphanages came to be created early on, even before the United States was created.

The first orphanage in what would eventually become the United States was established in New Orleans in 1727. King Louis XV of France had earlier commissioned the Catholic Order of the Ursulines to send a group of nuns to New Orleans to establish a school for girls where they would educate the daughters of French aristocracy and wealthy planters. In addition they were asked to teach casket girls (so named because of the "casques" or trunks in which they carried their belongings) who were sent from France in response to the need for marriageable girls in the predominantly male colony.

In 1727, Father de Beaubois, a missionary, asked the Ursuline nuns to accept and care for a young orphan girl whom he had removed from " a family with dissolute morals". Within the next 12 months they had accepted two other children. In describing her decision to accept the children, Mother Mary St. Augustin, the Superioress, said, "We have charged ourselves to provide these orphans with a suitable education which will enable them to earn their living according to their condition." It is not clear what this meant since in the early years the orphans got little more than religious training, manual labor chores, and housekeeping duty assignments.

This small nucleus was increased following an Indian massacre of French settlers in Natchez [Mississippi]. The Natchez Indians in a raid on the settlement had killed most of the men and taken the women and children captive. A French expedition sent from New Orleans was able to free the captives but was left with the problem of what to do with the liberated children, most of who were now orphans. French officials asked the Ursuline nuns to take the children, which they did. Exactly how many children were accepted at that time is not known but by 1731 the sisters were sheltering 49 homeless girls.

Initially the schooling provided to the orphans differed from that provided to the regular paying students in that the orphans were instructed primarily on housekeeping chores and other menial duties, while the regular students were educated in languages, communication skills, and other subjects considered appropriate for well-to-do young ladies of the day. However by the beginning of 19th century the Ursuline Convent had become well established as a refuge for homeless children and the nuns began to organize their orphanage program more formally, and early in the 19th century, reading, writing, arithmetic, French, and English had been added to the orphan children's curriculum. Through periods of expansion and shrinkage the Ursuline orphan program continued until 1824 when the city of New Orleans assumed responsibility, and all orphans were transferred to the Poydras Asylum - a government managed facility [it continues to this day, though now as a home for elderly women]. In 1839 the convent again began accepting orphan girls though the reason for this change of attitude is not clear. From 1840 to 1912 the sisters cared for 30-40 female orphans a year until 1912 when the Ursuline orphanage program was permanently shut down.

Not strictly a part of the developing "orphan home" issue but a closely related phenomenon was the program involving "orphan trains" in the mid to late 1800s in this country. As the number of homeless orphans and poor indigent children increased-primarily in the population centers on the East coast, especially Boston and New York City, what to do about them became an increasing public and political concern. They were accused of fostering prostitution and petty thievery (probably correctly so, but not necessarily by choice). Enterprising aid societies devised a solution which for a period of time benefited all concerned. Groups of orphans were collected at missions in the urban foci and shipped to western states where they were taken in by preselected rural families for whom they would provide much needed unskilled labor either on the farm or in the home. It was hoped by the organizers that the host families would eventually

adopt the orphans and make them an equal member of the family
- which in many cases they did. There was some abuse of the
program as one might expect, but for the most part it was
remarkably successful in reducing the burden of "street children"
in eastern urban centers, in supplying needed labor resource to
the rural westerners, and in providing badly deprived children
with the opportunity to grow up in a stable home environment
free from the evils of street life in the city.

This mass translocation of orphans from east coast cities to rural
farmlands in the west was effected through "orphan trains" as
they came to be known. Children were collected at a central
point, the organizing charity group would advertise their
availability in newspapers of western states such as Kansas,
Missouri, Indiana, Illinois etc., match the children with selected
families based on available data relating to need and
compatibility, and send them out by train, dropping off
individuals at predetermined destinations along the way. As few
as five or as many as 200 children might be loaded on a train
depending on need. Attempts were made to follow up on the
outplaced children at later dates to see if there had been a
successful merger between child and family but such efforts
were often inadequate. Among the major aid societies involved
in the "orphan train" program were the Boston Children's
Mission, the New York Children's Aid Society, the New York
Foundling Hospital, and the Philadelphia Women's Industrial
Aid Society. Between them, these groups translocated over
200,000 children during the life of the program. The program
dwindled in the late 19th century and ended by about 1912,
largely because the need for imported labor had decreased and
the public's concern that this was not far from indentured
servitude if not outright slavery. Many states passed laws
banning the importation/exportation of orphans or state
dependents and this effectively ended the program.

In Georgia, the first orphanage was the Ebenezer (originally Jerusalem) Orphanage built by the Lutheran Salzbergers who had emigrated from Austria in 1736 to escape religious persecution and who settled just north of Savannah in Effingham County. During the Civil War the orphanage and much of the town of New Ebenezer were destroyed in Sherman's March to the Sea in December 1864.

The second orphanage in Georgia and also located in the Savannah area was originally identified as simply "The Orphan House". Conceived as a "House of Mercy" by Charles Wesley, the great Methodist leader, and encouraged by General Oglethorpe, Georgia Colony founder, it remained for George Whitefield and James Habersham to actually bring the home to fruition. Whitefield first arrived in America in 1733 as Curate of the Church of England. On seeing the large number of children in the colony left destitute by death or desertion of family he resolved to find some relief for these unfortunate souls. Whitefield made several trips back to England to raise support for the children and petitioned English authorities for assistance. In lieu of a salary, he was granted 500 acres on which to establish his orphanage. In 1740 he returned to the Georgia Colony to begin the construction of the new orphanage. He and Habersham devoted much of their time and effort to erecting, supporting and expanding the new orphan home. An interesting historical note: Benjamin Franklin, who greatly admired Whitefield, tried in vain to persuade him to build the orphanage in Philadelphia rather than Georgia, but he would not. Though initially angered by Whitefield's refusal to move to Philadelphia, Franklin eventually relented and lent his support to the Georgia site.

Apparently the original Home was an impressive structure. Built ten miles outside of the then existing town, it was the largest building in the colony, a cause for some criticism since during its construction it was accused of "swallowing up" all of the tradesmen, laborers and materials available in the colony.

Established as a boy's home in 1740 and named Bethesda (House of Mercy) it has survived to this date and is the oldest surviving orphanage in the United States.

Both the Bethesda Boy's Home and the Ebenezer Orphanage relied heavily on agricultural crops raised by the children and in fact came to be considered the first two agricultural vocational schools in the state. They concentrated on production of rice, cotton, indigo, and silk (mulberry trees and silkworms), crops, which were suited to the area.

It was in the post-Civil War era that the Decatur United Methodist Children's Home (UMCH) was conceived and birthed, largely in response to a need created by the war. The Civil War had left huge numbers of orphaned and abandoned children wandering rootless and homeless about the countryside surviving as best they could. In a land already devastated by war there was little help available from the survivors on whose lands they trespassed. While sympathetic to their plight, the landowners could hardly support themselves let alone provide for the wandering bands of homeless. It was in this environment that one Georgia Methodist minister determined something must be done to alleviate the suffering of these children. Dr. Jesse Boring was, however, not just any Methodist minister. He was a devout Methodist, a determined reformer, a zealot, and an orator of considerable renown. And perhaps most of all he was a compassionate individual who could not ignore the plight of the homeless children all around him.

In 1869 Dr. Boring proposed to the North Georgia Conference of the Methodist Church that it support an orphanage which might help alleviate the pain and suffering of the homeless child victims of the Civil War. Boring was not alone in his recognition of a need for help for the children. Another prominent Methodist, Mr. J. W. McAfee from Payne Memorial Methodist Church in

Atlanta, decided that Dr. Boring was right to agitate for the establishment of a children's home and so added his encouragement and support. McAfee and several of his friends donated $100 each to Boring for his home and assured him of their continuing support in this endeavor.

To do justice to a history of the UMCH and its founder, Jesse Boring, it is necessary to give a fuller account of the Boring family in Georgia and detail some of the events leading up to the proposal by Dr. Boring for the establishment of a children's home in Georgia.

~ 2 ~

The Boring Family History

T he Boring family history has been traced back to the mid 18th century beginning with the birth of Isaac Boring March 8, 1762. Isaac and his wife, Phoebe Browning settled in Shiloh (Jackson County, Georgia) where they raised several children including a son John. The Borings were a Christian, patrician family, well educated and well respected in the community. Isaac Boring died on May 18, 1831, at the age of 79. His son John grew up in Shiloh where he became a Methodist preacher, educator, and superintendent of the first county school; he also conducted the first Methodist Sunday School in Georgia. He was married to the former Sarah Candler.

At this time, early in the 19th century, the state of Georgia, now 12 years old, was expanding to the west at a rapid rate. As new territory was acquired from the indigenous Creek and Cherokee Indians, new counties were created, land was raffled off to new immigrants, usually about 250 acres per parcel, and every effort was made to encourage raffle winners to settle permanently in the new county bringing increased trade, agriculture, and business to the new frontier. The opening of a new frontier county with the attendant land lottery was regarded as a fine opportunity for tradesmen, farmers, storekeepers, and business persons of all types to come in and provide for the needs of homesteaders and become part of the expanding civilization.

John Boring recognized this expansion of Georgia to the West as an opportunity to serve as an educator as well as a preacher in the new area, and when, in 1818, Gwinnett County was created just to the west of his home county of Jackson, he entered the land lottery and was granted a parcel of land in the new county. He moved his family into the Sweetwater Creek area of western Gwinnett County in what is now the town of Lilburn (not to be confused with the Sweetwater Creek in Manchester, Georgia, west of Atlanta which gained fame when the town was totally eradicated by General Sherman during the Civil War). Boring is described as an active, well-respected citizen who did his share to bring civilization into the new territory. That he was a civic minded active participant in his new home is suggested by the county records which show that in September 1823 he and two others were commissioned to lay out a new county road between Lawrenceville and the DeKalb County line. And again in March 1828 he and several others were appointed to construct a bridge across Sweetwater Creek on the main road from Decatur to Lawrenceville. By any measure, John Boring, like his father before him, was a success, an educated man, and a credit to his community.

His children seem to have been similarly productive. Two of them, Jesse and brother Isaac, both ultimately became Methodist preachers and medical doctors. A third son, Thomas, also became an active Methodist preacher, but not, apparently a physician.

Jesse Boring and the Children's Home

Jesse Boring was born the second son of John and Sarah in Jackson County on December 4, 1807, and moved with his family to newly created Gwinnett County as a young child. He joined the Methodist Church at the age of seven and shortly thereafter determined that he should become a Methodist preacher. At the age of 15 he was provisionally accepted into the Methodist ministry and was permitted to accompany Reverend William J. Parks, a circuit rider minister on the Chattahoochee River circuit; a route that was 300 miles long and reached into three states. (In early colonial days it was common practice, because of scant populations and long distances between

12

settlements, to use circuit-riding preachers who would travel from settlement to settlement ministering to the communities that could not support a full-time preacher and church. Such visits by a preacher to a community were often a month or more between calls.)

Jesse Boring's ministerial career got off to a slow and somewhat dubious beginning. As a youth he was extremely timid and given to stuttering and stammering to the extent that often he could not read in front of the congregation. Unable to read the Bible or sing hymns in church, he showed little promise as a future leader in the Methodist Church. Indeed, in his first job as a circuit rider, unsympathetic elders in the church encouraged him to give up his fledgling attempts at the ministry and go home to Gwinnett County and pursue some other occupation. Fortunately, Elishu Calloway, a senior member of the church and a mentor to young Boring, and W. J. Parks, his pastor, encouraged him to continue his studies and preaching, which he did, ultimately to become one of Methodism's greatest orators.

Between 1827 and 1830, Boring served the church in various assignments including Tallahassee, Milledgeville, and LaGrange. In 1830, suffering from ill health he was remanded to Milledgeville where he spent the next three years assigned to "less strenuous duties". He then moved to Alabama where he spent several more years in semi-retirement because of his continuing health problems.

It seems incongruous that a person with such boundless energy for his chosen work should be so constrained by health problems, but for all his enthusiasm, Boring was severely handicapped throughout most of his life by his physical frailties. While he regained his strength after the Alabama respite, he was never a physically strong person. Later in life (1871) he would be permanently crippled in a railroad accident. As he stepped off the train in Opelika, Alabama, while traveling from Columbus, Georgia, to Atlanta on the Montgomery and West Point Railroad, he fell into an eight-foot ditch and was severely

13

injured. In a suit filed against the railroad in Opelika, he was awarded $10,000.00 and expenses – a princely sum at that time.

On October 26, 1833, he married Harriet E. Howard in Columbus, Georgia. She was 17 and he was 26. He continued to serve as a Methodist minister in the Georgia- Alabama area until 1849 when he was selected by Bishop Robert Paine to introduce and establish southern Methodism to the Territory of California. He accompanied the gold rush prospectors to California where he served the church in various capacities. In 1855 he left California (now a state) and returned to Georgia where he enrolled in medical school, graduating from the Atlanta Medical College (now a part of Emory University) in 1858.

That same year he was sent, along with Hamilton G. Horton, a fellow minister, to Texas where Boring would minister in San Antonio. His companion would go on to serve in Uvalde, Texas, about 60 miles west of San Antonio. Horton describes some of their experiences. He and Boring left Georgia in 1858, landed in Galveston, Texas, later that year and continued westward in an old four horse stagecoach. Approaching the Colorado River, which they had to cross, they were told by a local blacksmith that they could not proceed, as "the mud was so soft and deep that a buzzard flying twenty feet above the ground, his shadow would bog him down". Horton goes on to describe his first preaching assignment en route to Uvalde. This was in the Butcher Dillard settlement where he conducted a revival meeting in a dirt floored cottage "with rifles and shotguns stacked in the corners and pistols and Bowie knives around our waists ... women as well as men, and with the worshippers keeping an eye out the window throughout the service to ensure their horses were not stolen by Indians as they prayed." When Horton reached Uvalde he found it consisted of a small group of log houses, each house with port holes to shoot at marauding Indians. The upper floor of the jailhouse served as the courtroom as well as the church. This evoked the comment from one irreverent parishioner that "when you were in jail you were in church, and when you were in church you were in jail."

Boring, assigned in San Antonio, not only pastored churches but also, along with his son Nicholas, helped to establish a medical school there and both men served on its faculty. Not content with these contributions, Jesse and others of the Boring family also started a women's college in San Antonio, which ultimately evolved into the present day Trinity University.

Meanwhile in the East, severe political and social unrest were developing. By 1860 it was clear that differences between southern slaveholders and northern abolitionists would soon lead to open conflict. Jesse Boring was an ardent anti-abolitionist. His father and other kin had been slaveholders in Georgia and though Jesse had none, he believed it was wrong for the government to interfere and tell slave owners that they must free their slaves. He preached that he would prefer the country remain as one and that differences between the North and South be worked out peaceably, but in the event this was not possible then he supported the slave owners and secession from the Union. In 1860 Boring joined the Confederate Army as physician and chaplain in General H. C. McCullough's division serving in Texas and Arkansas. Little information is available concerning his activities during the war.

Following the war, in 1868, Boring returned to Georgia where he served as presiding elder of the Atlanta, LaGrange, and Augusta districts. In those years immediately after the war, Georgia and other southern states in particular, were in economic, cultural, political, and social chaos. Families were separated, people were homeless, starving and without hope. Worst of all perhaps were the bands of roving children with no families and little food and clothing, trying to survive in the midst of this turmoil. A man of compassion, Boring could not ignore the sad predicament of the orphaned and abandoned children. He began almost immediately upon his return to Georgia to agitate for some action by the Methodist Church to rectify the plight of the children. The first published reference to the need for an orphanage in North Georgia appeared in the October 1869 issue of the Southern Christian Advocate in an article authored by Jesse Boring.

15

By the time of the 1869 North Georgia Annual Conference Boring had convinced most members of the need to provide for the orphans of Georgia and particularly those of the North Georgia Conference area. As a result of his impassioned pleas, the Conference resolved to take action immediately to establish an orphan home. A special committee was appointed to establish the orphanage in North Georgia. That same year six generous Methodists, John Thrasher, Givens Arnold, George Jones, Thomas Boring, and Messrs. McElroy and Lively agreed to purchase from Thomas Jones (unrelated to George Jones) a site for the orphanage at a price of $6,000. The land was located in Gwinnett County in the vicinity of present day Norcross. They actually paid about $1,000 down and signed a note for the remaining $5,000. They then presented the encumbered title to the newly appointed Board of Trustees who had been charged by the Conference to create and oversee the operation of the future Home. The Board, comprised of six Methodist clergymen and six lay leaders, immediately set about drawing up the guidelines for the proposed orphanage.

The donated tract consisted of approximately 619 acres on which was one large eight-room house and three smaller houses. The land was considered well suited for agricultural use being especially well suited for the production of cereal grains, grasses, and cotton. A plentiful supply of water was available on the land.

Dr. Jesse Boring was appointed agent (fund raiser and financial manager) of the newly created orphanage while his brother Thomas and wife were appointed supervisor (operational manager) and matron respectively. The supervisor's job was to oversee operation of the home and manage the farm. The matron's job was to tend to the needs of the children and the home proper.

While firmly committed to the development of the orphanage in Norcross to serve the North Georgia Conference, Boring did not limit himself to that program. He was also largely responsible for the establishment of a second Methodist orphanage in

Georgia, this one in the South Georgia Conference. It was established two years after the North Georgia orphanage and was located in Macon Georgia (where it remains to this day). Its beginning was not unlike the Norcross home in that it started with a donation of 94 acres of land and a 10 room house.

Boring continued in one role or another to serve the Methodist Church for many years. He was a presiding elder in Atlanta and Griffin districts in the 1870s, and the pastor of St. John's Methodist Church in Augusta in 1880. His last assignments were in the Athens, Newnan, and Augusta districts. He was retired at the North Georgia Conference in Augusta in 1886 but continued to serve the church until two weeks before his death in early 1890 at his brother's South Georgia home in Dixie. He was 83 years old. At his request he was buried on the grounds of the Methodist Children's Home in Decatur which had meant so much to him in life. His remains are there today near the entrance to the administration building marked with a headstone bearing the quote, " He who turns a child to God changes the course of history."

~ 3 ~

The Difficult Early Years (1871-1880)

The North Georgia Conference acting under the insistent prodding of Jesse Boring, had in 1869 taken the initial steps to establish an orphan home in the general area of Atlanta. The Home was located in the present day Norcross area and consisted of approximately 619 acres on which were several buildings, most importantly the large eight room house that would be the first home for the orphan children. With certain internal modifications the Home had a capacity for 25-30 children. As proof of need, children were not long in coming to the Home. The first child accepted was a seven-year-old girl named Donie (Donnie?) Anderson about whom little else is known.

By the time of the official dedication of the Home on April 26, 1871, there were already 19 children (15 girls and 4 boys) living there. The dedication of the orphanage at Norcross was the occasion of much local interest. A large crowd of southern notables gathered at 11 a.m. in a grove near the Home for the ceremony which began with the orphans singing, followed by prayers and speeches. In addition to the Methodist speakers, a major participant was one Cincinnatus Peeples, a Baptist, included to show that it was not the intent to limit the Home to Methodists but rather to accept individuals from any faith that met the criteria of need which had been established by the Trustees.

Though the Home was dedicated in April, it was not until November 21st of that year that an official charter was granted by

19

the State of Georgia. (See appendix for complete copy of the charter.)

Essential to the Home's success was the development of a farm which could provide at least some of the food for the orphans and some cash crops which could be sold to help with the Home's expenses. The first year's production was disappointing to the Superintendent but still yielded 55 bushels of corn, 3000 bundles of fodder, 2 1/2 tons of hay, 2 bales of cotton, and a goodly crop of potatoes and turnips. Not too bad for a new farm operation with most of the labor provided by untrained small children. That same year a large number of fruit trees of different varieties were planted.

At the time of the first report of the Orphan's Home by the Trustees at the meeting of the North Georgia Conference in December 1871 there were 33 orphans in the Home and over 100 others had applied but been rejected for one reason or another, primarily for a lack of space. At the same meeting, plans were laid out for increasing the capacity of the Home so that more children could be accommodated. Dr. Boring reported that he had received $42,608 in cash, land and subscriptions during the first year.

Shortly, however, the land donors found themselves unable to meet the payments due on the original loan and the seller filed suit to recover his land. The donors, seller, and Trustees met and agreed to resolve the debt by deeding clear title for 100 acres to the Trustees of the Home and returning the remaining 519 acres back to the seller. On November 14, 1872, title for 100 acres of land was transferred from DeWitt Jones to the Trustees; cost was $1,130.

A new home building and a schoolhouse had been started and by November 1872 the schoolhouse had been completed and the home was about two-thirds complete. When finished the new house was expected to house about 60 children as well as the Superintendent and his family.

The first Agent (financial manager) appointed had been Dr. Jesse Boring; the first Superintendent (general manager) had been Dr. Thomas Boring; and the first Matron (child caretaker and teacher) was Mrs. Thomas Boring. Thomas Boring resigned as Superintendent in 1872 (as did his wife the Matron) and brother Jesse attempted to carry on in his place doing both the Superintendent and Agent jobs. Unfortunately ill health forced Jesse to resign after a few months. The Trustees then hired the Reverend W. R. Foote as Superintendent as of July 5, 1872. This instability in the superintendency position at a time when farming duties were critical to the Home resulted in a poor year for the farm operation. The crop production for the year 1872 was recorded as: 20 bushels of wheat, 60 bushels of oats, 50 bushels of corn, 3 bales of cotton, 20 bushels of peas, and 100 bushels of potatoes.

In addition to the Agent, Superintendent, and Matron, the Trustees hired a teacher, Mrs. L. A. Rogers, and two assistants, Misses Sallie Crittenden and Eliza Gibson. These latter two ladies would instruct the girls in the domestic arts and economics of housekeeping.

On Friday, April 26, 1872, the second anniversary of the orphanage was celebrated at the Home near Norcross. It was a festive occasion. Colonel Sage, Superintendent of the Atlanta and Richmond Railroad (a local rail line), announced he would furnish a special train to carry celebrants to the Home and would have cars sufficient to transport 500 persons at the nominal sum of 30 cents per passenger round trip – Atlanta to Norcross and back.

Should Sunday Schools or other groups wish, he was prepared to provide them with a private car for $14.00. He announced that all persons going would be provided with an abundant basket dinner and an ample supply of the best water. However, he also suggested that travelers carry a large basket filled with food. Whether this last was intended to provide the orphans with a bonus banquet or was to ensure that the guests really did have enough to eat was not clear in his announcement.

In spite of its early success, the orphanage in Norcross soon ran into a number of problems which are not well described in the recorded history but the troubles reached a climax in 1873 when a fire severely damaged the facility. A statement in the 1873 report to the North Georgia Conference stated that "the location near Norcross ... was found on trial to be completely unacceptable." Accordingly, the Norcross facility was abandoned and the Trustees bought, for $6,000, a new property, 218 acres on Snapfinger Road (now Columbia Drive) near Decatur and moved the orphanage. The change of location was reported to be a positive improvement and was described as "in all respects beneficial to the interests of the Home, and the Trustees are satisfied that in the economical point of view a great advantage has been gained by transferring the Home to Decatur."

Of the new purchase, 70 acres were virgin forest. The remaining acreage was for the most part well suited for farming and had on it one large two story home along with several lesser buildings. The large two-story house was quickly modified to serve as the children's home with the girl's dormitory on one side and the boy's on the other across the hall. A kitchen and dining room occupied an ell at the rear and a narrow porch extended the full length across the front of the building. Much of the credit for the rapid and extensive modifications to the house must go to the Atlanta and Decatur church congregations which contributed so unstintingly to prepare the Home for the children. The superintendent at the new Decatur facility was the Reverend R. W. Foote who had moved with the children from the Norcross facility. Superintendent Foote made numerous improvements at the new Decatur property in its first year of operation. He was particularly concerned that the farm component be made to produce crops as soon as possible. Three hundred fruit trees were set out that first year as were a number of grape vines. Fences and buildings were repaired and a truly productive farm was created.

In its first year of operation in Decatur the farm facility yield included: 5 bales of cotton, 310 bushels of corn, 4000 pounds of fodder, 200 bushels of potatoes, plus peas and other vegetables. This was done with only the help of one hired farm worker, the staff, and the children of the Home.

There were only six salaried employees at the Home - Superintendent Foote, Agent Cook, Matron Foote, and her assistant, one teacher, and one skilled farm laborer. The total payroll was $1,550 for that year.

Children coming into the Home in these early years were, for the most part, under educated, under disciplined, and under trained in the social graces as compared with their peers. They had, after all, been living without one or both parents and were often learned only in how to survive in an uncaring, inhospitable world. Under the able tutelage of Mr. and Mrs. Foote and teacher Sallie Crittenden, the children learned quickly. In addition to academic skills they made great strides in personal appearance, habits, morals, and religion – far better than had been anticipated by the Trustees.

The Superintendent, ever seeking economic relief, organized a program whereby clothing for the orphans would be provided by Sunday Schools, churches, and Aid Societies in the area. The children were taught school on the campus and attended Sunday School at the First Methodist Church in Decatur.

In 1874 the Trustees decided to merge the two jobs of Superintendent and Agent into one position with Mr. Foote assuming both roles. The basis for this change was that financial problems necessitated cutting expenses wherever possible and because of his demonstrated ability it was felt that Mr. Foote could successfully assume both roles and thus save the Home the cost of one salary.

This year the farm produced 150 bushels of corn, 3300 pounds of fodder, 8 bales of cotton, and other field and garden crops. The farm also acquired some livestock: one mule, 12 head of cattle and 10 hogs.

By 1875 there were 32 children, 18 girls and 14 boys. Of the 32 children, 27 had become members of the Methodist Church since entering the Home. Of the remaining five, two had only recently arrived and the other three were too young to be accepted into the church on profession of faith. That the children should enter into the church was an important objective of the Home staff and the Trustees who expressed great satisfaction with the acceptance of the children into the church.

Over the next two years growth of the Home continued. The children continued to learn in all areas and to develop wholesome character. They were industrious, happy, and in general a source of great satisfaction to their mentors. The Trustees recognized a need to improve the level of formal education taught to the children and proposed giving them a proper English education (whatever that might be) but they found this was not practicable. Much of the boys' time was necessarily spent working on the farm and the older boys also worked off the campus on neighboring farms to earn a part of their livelihood and thus relieve some of the stress on Home finances. Because of the limited time available for school, they received an imperfect education. The Home did secure the services of a Miss Clara Pierce as an additional teacher and with her help they were able to show some improvement in the children's education.

One major problem faced by the Home was a lack of space for housing the children. The administrators were regularly forced to reject children because there was no space for them to live. Plans were drawn up for a four-room addition to be added to the dwelling house. This would serve as a residence for the Superintendent and his family and make more space available for the children.

In spite of the success of the farm and the salary savings instituted by the Superintendent, the Home still was having financial difficulties and was barely able to meet daily expenses - not saving any money to pay off the land debt. This debt burden would be a continuing problem for several years and a source of great concern for the Trustees.

An interesting side note: J. G. Foote, son of Superintendent Foote, met, courted, and married one of the girls from the Home "a queenly girl of fine ancestry" as reported by one contemporary writer.

Mr. Foote served as agent/supervisor for three years (1874-1876) and on his retiring, exhausted by the work, the Trustees again divided the work into two positions - agent and supervisor, as it had been earlier. Dr. W. B. Scott was appointed as Agent and the Reverend J. L. Lupo was named Superintendent. These two were to serve in their respective roles until 1880 when Scott would be replaced as agent by the Reverend Sam Jones, though Lupo would continue to serve as Superintendent until 1882.

The lack of financial support given the Home by churches in the North Georgia Conference eventually reached crisis proportions and in 1876 the Trustees reported at the North Georgia Conference : "...the orphans home does not fully meet the urgent necessity that prompted its foundation." That is, it was falling short of filling the needs of the destitute orphan children of North Georgia. With a realistic capacity of only 25-30 orphans, a several fold increase in living space was needed if it was to fulfil its obligation to the Church and society. The Trustees took the Methodist Church to task saying that it had accepted the responsibility for creating a home for needy children but the Church was not keeping faith in meeting this responsibility. They pointed out that it was too late to consider this an experiment that could now be terminated as impractical; rather it was a viable reality and now must be supported appropriately. They estimated that about $1,000 per annum would feed, clothe, and educate 25 children at the Home. The Trustees pled with the Conference ministers to return to their congregations and aggressively solicit adequate support for the Home.

By the end of 1878 it was agreed that the Home could comfortably accommodate a maximum 25 children, and

25

meanwhile efforts would continue to try to provide additional living quarters. In fact, there were only 19 children living at the Home at the time of the 1878 report, in part because finances as well as space were limiting factors. Nevertheless a goal of 50 children was set as a reasonable objective to meet the true need. The board felt that if the current real estate depression would abate, then the assets of the Home would, for the first time since its inception, exceed its liabilities. The overall indebtedness had been reduced that year to about $10,000.

In 1879 Agent Scott was able to secure enough money to reduce the debt on the Home slightly. However by 1880 the money problem was again critical. That year net income totaled $1,288 in cash and $247 in materials, while expenses for the year were less than $900. Agent Scott believed that in the next year annual expenses could be further reduced to about $700. Unfortunately at this same time, land values had been falling for several years and the net value of the Home was assessed at $8,900 while the total debt was $9,645. Some salaries were not being paid fully or on time. In short, the Home was bankrupt. The Trustees agreed that in the coming year they must either materially reduce the debt burden or close the children's home completely. The latter course they considered unacceptable. They again pleaded with all the preachers in the conference to redouble their efforts to secure support from their congregations.

Finances not withstanding, the Home was doing reasonably well. A severe drought had reduced farm yields below expectations, but with only one hired worker the farm produced that year: 7 bales of cotton, 350 bushels of wheat, 125 gallons of syrup, and a good crop of potatoes and vegetables. The livestock (cattle and hogs) were in fine condition and increasing in numbers.

The orphan population was 21 at the end of 1879 including eleven boys and ten girls, ages from six to sixteen and one girl of 21 who had grown up in the Home and stayed on to teach the younger children.

~ 4 ~

Early Leaders and Expansion Years
(1881-1900)

I n 1876 the Reverend J. L. Lupo had been appointed
Superintendent replacing Mr. Foote. Lupo continued to
serve in this post into the early 1880s with W. C. Scott
acting as Agent through most of those same years. During
their joint tenure the Home's financial status began to improve.

Dr. Lupo was locally regarded as "the best farmer in DeKalb
County" and the farm output during his tenure supports that as
factual. He increased output each year, even including the
drought years of 1880 and 1881.

However, even with his ability as a farmer, Dr. Lupo (and Agent
Scott) was not able to eliminate or significantly reduce the heavy
indebtedness burdening the Home. In fact, finances were so
unstable that many in the church, and outsiders as well, began to
look on the Home as an embarrassment and an albatross which
could best be discarded. Recognizing the severity of the financial
crisis, Bishop McTyeire at the December 1880 conference in
Rome, asked the Reverend Sam Jones if he would assume the
responsibility as Agent for the Home and attempt to salvage it
before others forced its dissolution. Jones was selected for this
particular job, at least in part, because of his reputation as an
outstanding fundraiser. He was, in fact, far more than a
fundraiser. He was among the best-known Methodist evangelists
in the country, certainly in the South. The energy with which

Jones attacked the financial problem and his success at resolving it are well described in his biography written by his wife in 1906. *(The Life and Sayings of Sam P. Jones* by Laura Jones; Franklin-Turner Co. Publishers). A contemporary article in the *Atlanta Constitution* says, "We have never commended a more admirable charity than the Orphans' Home" and goes on to praise Sam Jones for making it all possible. Jones's activities made 1881 an outstanding one for the Home financially. During this year the indebtedness of the Home was reduced by $2,100 and stood in December at $7,522. Total assets of the

Rev. Sam P. Jones, Agent 1880-1891; Superintendent 1882-1895

Home were valued at $9,000 giving the Home a positive cash value for the first time since its inception – not a grand financial success but a strong step towards insuring its survival.

An interesting aside on Jones: A Captain Tom Ryman from Nashville, Tennessee, owner and operator of several steamships on the Cumberland River, attended a three week long revival led by Jones and in the process became an enthusiastic convert to Christianity and specifically to Methodism. He tried to persuade Jones to settle or locate in a Nashville church but Jones declined to move from his home in Cartersville, Georgia, from which he felt he could more comfortably travel the southeast evangelizing. Ryman then decided that if Jones was going to insist on staying in Cartersville, then he was going to live in a home more suited to a person of his considerable stature and he had an entire new floor added to the Jones home replete with all the trimmings of a classic opulent Victorian home. That home still stands in

Cartersville today and is now a museum to the Jones family owned and operated by the county. Ryman went on to build a city auditorium in Nashville. He called it the Jones-Ryman Auditorium to further honor Sam Jones. In later years it became world famous as home to the Grand Old Opry of country music fame and eventually the name was shortened to simply the Ryman Auditorium.

The farm continued to be productive during the 1800s in spite of an ongoing drought, and no serious problems occurred during these years either on campus or with the children. At this time there were 20 children in residence.

In 1882 Superintendent Lupo resigned, much to the regret of trustee administrators as well as the Home staff and the children. He was replaced by the Rev. P. G. Turner. Rev. Sam Jones remained as Agent.

The whole decade of the 1880s was unquestionably one of the best for the Home up to that time. By the end of 1882 the Home's indebtedness had been reduced to $3800. At the same time, the number of children in residence had increased to 35 with every available bed occupied and no space to accept additional applicants (of which there were many).

The 1883 Trustees report stated that the Home was "no longer a questionable experiment" but was now a permanently established enterprise of the North Georgia Conference. Much credit for turning the Home into a reality was given not only to the Supervisors, Agents, and their staffs, but also to one V.R. Tommey, who, as a member of the Board of Trustees had on numerous occasions used his personal funds during these critical years to meet the financial obligations when the Home could not do so. But for his personal financial assistance and his influence over others to lend their support, the Home would almost certainly have succumbed to debt, been closed and the children scattered during the early 1880s.

At the end of 1883 there were 33 children in the Home and a commitment made to accept another eight making a total of 41 in all. Because it seemed that growth would likely continue for some time to come, plans were drawn up for a new building which could house up to three times the present number of residents.

The new residence building, first proposed in 1884, was completed and occupied the following year and the main portion of the old building was moved up to join with the rear of the new house. Rooms in the new building were furnished at a cost of $75 each and rooms in the older section were refurbished at a cost of $50 each. The new building, reflecting the powerful influence of Agent Jones (and in fact owing its very existence to the ability of Jones to raise funds for its construction), came to be known familiarly as the "Sam Jones Orphanage". By the end of 1885 there were 35 children, 18 boys and 17 girls living in the new facility. Their ages ranged from 3 to 17 years.

Without doubt, the most significant milestone for the decade occurred in 1883 when, for the first year since its inception, the Home was declared to be "debt-free". The significance which the trustees attached to achieving a "debt-free status" is evident in their annual reports in which for several years (1883, 1885 and1887) the reports proudly declared that the Home was at last out of debt. After so many precarious years with debts threatening imminent closure it seems that the trustees themselves were in awe that the Home was at last financially secure.

By 1886 there were 40 children in residence, all were healthy and well cared for and the Home was continuing to improve its financial state. By this time too, children were beginning to "graduate" from the Home as they reached the "age of independence". Basically the age of independence meant upon completion of high school – the age at which their peers commonly would be expected to leave home and seek outside employment. For girls it also could mean the age at which they married. One of the girl graduates was now enrolled in LaGrange

Female College about 30 miles away and another was now happily married.

The farm suffered this year from a continuing drought and production of most crops was reduced significantly although the wheat crop fared well apparently because of its favored location and extra care afforded it.

By 1887 the orphan population had increased to 45 thanks to the additional living quarters which had been added. Much new farm equipment and some livestock had been purchased to support growth of the essential and financially successful farm component. New sewing machines had been purchased to help the girls with their domestic work. That same year, Mr. Thomas Holleyman was appointed Superintendent, succeeding Reverend F. M. T. Brannon though the indefatigable Sam Jones continued in his capacity as Agent. In what had become and was to remain a common trend, the trustees appointed Rev. Brannon's wife as Matron, a policy which allowed a sharing of managerial duties with each spouse pursuing those activities for which he/she was best suited while at the same time insuring a close coordination between the activities of the two managers.

The years 1888 and 1889 were copies of 1887 with the managerial staff continuing as before and Agent Sam Jones continuing to secure the necessary funds. A new school house/chapel building was completed and opened in January 1889. Work begun the year before continued on the construction of a new main building which would provide increased living quarters for the children. As the Home continued to grow and the fiscal needs increased, it became necessary to employ a second agent. Especially since Rev. Jones was absent much of the time on evangelical tours there was a need for an agent representative to be at the Home constantly. The Reverend Howard L. Crumley was engaged as Assistant Agent in 1890. The choice of these two men as financial providers was clearly a stroke of unbelievably good fortune for the Home. Jones served as Agent or Supervisor for over 12 years and Mr. Crumley served as Assistant Agent or Agent for at least 19 years including those as assistant to Jones. During their collective tenure they were more successful at providing for the financial needs of the Home than any of their predecessors and, in some ways, their successors.

Also in 1888, the young lady and former Home resident (Miss Wing) who had attended LaGrange College for the previous three years returned after completing her studies and became a teacher for the children at the Home.

With the Home now comfortably established as a secure entity, more attention could now be focused on administrative matters. The number of trustees (who ultimately were responsible for the Home) was reduced from twelve to three to make it a more manageable group. Also, where funding for the Home previously had come from many sources, most of them outside the North Georgia Conference, now efforts were begun to insure that funding was derived primarily, if not exclusively, from within the North Georgia Conference where it properly belonged. In 1891 Agents Jones and Crumley succeeded for the first time in securing all funds from within the North Georgia Conference which has since that time been the major source for funds excepting those received from governmental sources.

The next several years continued along the same lines as those of the 1880s. There were 41 resident orphans at the end of 1892. As the children grew older (the Home by 1892 had served the children for 20 years) there developed a growing need and desire to provide advanced education - beyond the high school level- for those who wanted to continue with their academics and who were capable of competing successfully with their peers.

In 1891 the Reverend Sam Jones, after serving 12 years as Agent, retired from the Home and was replaced by his assistant, H.L. Crumley. The new resident teacher was Miss Maggie Dickenson. The country was suffering from a general depression at that time but Crumley was still able to collect enough funds to ensure another successful worry-free year.

In the year 1892 the Agnes Scott Seminary (later Agnes Scott College) agreed to provide a thorough education for one female student each year at no cost to the Home. Unidentified benefactors provided for the training of another orphan in the State Industrial School - specific training not identified - and two other benefactors agreed to support training at the Southern School for Shorthand for a third child.

The new resident teacher, appointed in 1892, was a Miss Ruth Hollyman. Teachers often did not stay long in the Home program. For the most part they were young, fresh out of school themselves, often little older than some of the children they taught. Perhaps they were intimidated by students almost their age - there has been some suggestion that this may have been true in some instances. This, and the fact that often these young ladies entered into their profession with idealistic dreams of how they could improve the world through teaching but were not prepared to deal with the reality of their jobs. In any case, it was not unusual for the young teachers to leave the teaching program after only a few months or a year or two.

In 1892 and 1893 the physical facility of the Home was again enlarged and improved. An addition was built onto the main building which add-on contained on the ground floor, a 24x36 foot-dining hall and on the upstairs level, a boys dormitory with two baths. The additional housing allowed for more children. During these same years the farm also did well, producing more than it ever had in earlier years.

There were 42 children in the Home in December 1895, ranging in age from 4 to 18 years – 22 girls and 20 boys.

Plans were drawn up this year for celebration of the 25th anniversary of the Home in 1896. The big fete was hosted at the Home in 1896 with local rail lines providing transportation for dignitaries coming from the city of Atlanta to Decatur. The trustees took advantage of the gathering to exhort attendees to support the Home in a more generous fashion. They especially asked for special funding of $3,000 for building expansion. So well subscribed was their request (they received over $6,000) that in short order a new boys building was constructed without any debt being incurred. The building could house 50 boys and a matron (housemother). The year ended with 56 children in residence, 22 girls and 34 boys. That year, even with the increased space they still rejected another 60 applicants. The insistent plea for funds which had been made to the congregations of the North Georgia Conference had been answered with more and more dollars thereby easing the financial concerns, but it had also generated an increasing number of applications for child placement in the Home. The need for additional space and personnel continued much as before.

In 1897, responding to Agent Crumley's pleas, members of the North Georgia Conference contributed more to the Home than in any previous year. This in spite of the fact that as Crumley reported, he was able to visit only about one-fourth of the congregations in the Conference. He had been able to stimulate the respective church leaders to the extent that they were able to solicit support even though he was unable to meet personally with the memberships. Thus ended the decade, a period of healthy growth, of financial stability, of enlarged and improved facilities, and of general satisfaction to all concerned.

~ 5 ~

The 20th Century, First Quarter (1901-1925)

The first quarter of the 20th century (1901-1925) was a particularly good time for the Methodist Children's Home. Excepting a brief period in 1917-1918 when World War 1 created short-lived shortages in many areas (food, personnel and materials), the early 1900s saw rapid growth and development of activities at the Home. The number of children in residence as well as the number outplaced to good homes increased; the physical facility, both farm and housing areas, were enlarged and improved; the financial status, though never seeming adequate, was no major issue during this period; in short, this was a very positive period for the Home.

During the years between 1901 and 1925 funding for the Home increased steadily (See Table 3.) At the beginning of the new century the income (and for all practical purposes the expenses as well) was about $12,000.00 a year and by the end of the first quarter, in 1925, income amounted to over $27,00.00 a year and expenses were just over $21,000.00.

Accompanying the general growth during this period were a number of significant changes - elimination of outdated programs and facilities, modernization of existing programs, construction or installation of new facilities, and implementation of new concepts.

Among the innovations introduced during this period was the establishment of the Work Day. Conceived by W. F. Cruselle of the Atlanta Constitution, and approved by Howard L. Crumley,

Agent at the Home, Work Day was established as the one day in the calendar year when all churches in the North Georgia Conference encouraged their members to donate one day's wages to the Children's Home. The idea was well accepted by many congregations throughout the Conference and the Work Day donation quickly became an important source of funds for the annual support of the Home. Sunday Schools found this project particularly appealing and it soon was unofficially established as a staple of Sunday School support with superintendents and their congregations earnestly soliciting extra monies for the Home on this date. It was not many years before the Work Day contributions became a major, and often the major, source of funds for maintenance of the Home. Work Day remains today an important source of funds for the day to day operation of the Home. Although exact dates may vary, Work Day is usually designated for a Sunday in October or late September.

A significant physical improvement for the Home in 1904 was the purchase and installation of a new gasoline engine connected to a water pump, and a pipe system laid which allowed fresh spring water to be pumped throughout the buildings including the laundry for cleaning and toiletry purposes. It was also pumped to the farm area for watering stock and cleaning. Drinking and cooking water for the cottages came from city wells and was provided by the city of Decatur at no cost to the Home (so long as consumption did not exceed an established amount of $25.00 a month).

Another important physical change made during this period was the replacement of the old inadequate boiler with a new, larger, and more efficient one. A seemingly minor change, it was of considerable importance to those who lived in the cottages especially during the winter months. The boiler provided heat for the buildings in cold weather, hot water for the laundry, and heat for use in the kitchen as well.

Home girls doing laundry.   About 1900

Blacksmith Shop built by Home boys.   About 1900

R.F. Shedden with girls preparing for a trip. Girls are tied together with string so they will not get separated. About 1912

The next major home improvement was the installation in 1906 of a new acetylene gas lighting system. Up until this time residents made do with kerosene lamps which provided marginal quality light and whose use created a constant fire risk. With the installation of the new acetylene system the residents now had better light at less risk. The acetylene apparatus consisted of a gas manufacturing chamber which was filled with calcium carbide and above which was suspended a large water tank. As water was metered into the gas manufacturing chamber, a chemical reaction between the water and the calcium carbide generated acetylene gas and sent it under its own pressure through a newly installed pipe system to light fixtures throughout the campus. (Such systems are nowhere in use today but an excellent example of one remains on public display *in situ* at the Biltmore House in Ashville, North Carolina.)

R.F. Shedden with the children. Date unknown

In August of 1909 the water tank and tower which had stored water and provided pressure for the Home for many years, collapsed. Fortunately it hit no one and did no damage to existing structures when it fell. It was replaced with a 50 foot tower and a 12,000 gallon water tank. With this greater capacity and pressure it was then possible to install larger water lines throughout the system and thereby better supply the Home with adequate water for cleaning and sanitation and to fight fires on campus; important since the Home was responsible for its own fire protection. Although the City of Decatur Fire Department could be summoned in an emergency, the time required for its wagons to travel from Decatur to the orphanage made calling on the Decatur Fire Department an exercise in futility since one could not expect them to arrive before the structure in question was completely consumed by fire.

A major building addition in 1906 was the building of a new on-campus chapel. On April 12, 1906, Bishop Candler of the North Georgia Conference laid the cornerstone for the new Moore

Chapel, funds for which had been donated largely by Mr. and Mrs. Thomas Moore of Bolton, Georgia. A marble slab just inside the door of the chapel identifies all of the donors. The Moore Chapel

Moore Chapel Built 1906

quickly became the showpiece for the Home (it still is). Not large, but adequate for the congregation it served, it was made of granite and had a series of most attractive stained glass windows. The large stained glass window behind the pulpit depicting

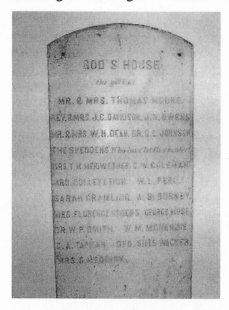

Plaque inside Moore Chapel identifying donors who contributed for its construction. 1906

Hoffman's "Christ Blessing the Children" was a special gift of the Bale family of Rome, Georgia. As originally furnished, it reportedly could seat 300 persons. Though the seats were small and adapted to the youthful population, it is still difficult to imagine seating 300 persons in this modest sized chapel. By 1920 the seating arrangement had been altered and the children's seats replaced by a lesser number of adult sized chairs. More recently this inferior seating was replaced by pews which comfortably seated a bit over 100 persons. This is the same seating that exists in the Chapel today. (Incidentally the chapel was used in the 1940s in the making of the Hollywood movie, *A Man Called Peter,* though it was not identified as the Children's Home's Moore Chapel in the movie.)

The original plan of the orphanage called for a single large building to house all of the children as well as offices, staff quarters, and an eating area. This was the design of the orphanage as originally established in Norcross, and this same concept was followed when the Home first moved to Decatur. However, by the turn of the century it was evident that the Home was outgrowing its housing capacity and in the early 1900s the single building concept was abandoned in favor of multiple "cottages" or residences with each one resembling the single family dwellings many of the children had known before entering the orphanage. Thus the building program was accelerated and in the late 19th and early 20th century several new cottages were constructed.

By 1920 there were seven cottages on the campus, Epworth Cottage (built in 1889), Gregg Cottage (1896), Hemphill Cottage (1903), Atlanta Cottage (1906), Martha Fort Williams Cottage (1910), Walton Cottage (1912), and Shedden Cottage (1911). Also there was the Hawkins Building- the main offices and dining room (1918), and various farm buildings including a new barn and two new 12 foot silos (1908). (See Chapter 11)

Fire was an ever present concern at the Home. Beginning with the burning of the original building in 1873 when the orphanage was located in Norcross and continuing through to today there is always the worry of fire, especially in the children's cottages. Both the Shedden and the Gregg cottages had suffered significant fires and had to be rebuilt. On June 5, 1918, a major fire broke out in what was then Fannie Dean Hall and gutted the frame building. This had housed the administrative offices, the kitchen and the dining room. Many records, portraits, and historic documents were destroyed in the fire. This building was replaced later in the year with the brick Hawkins Building. After

41

several serious fires at the Home, it became standard practice to build new buildings, especially any that would house children, out of brick or stone.

The children's placement in the cottages was (and is) dependent on their age and sex except that for many years all infants were usually housed in a single cottage. Young boys were housed in one cottage, older boys in another. Similarly young girls were housed in a separate cottage from older girls.

It is not really practical to go into detail as to what was the makeup of children assigned to a particular cottage because over the years the uses of the cottages changed, often several times. For example, Atlanta Cottage, originally built to house older girls later was used for younger girls as well. (In 1920 it housed 24 girls from 14 to 20 years old and 10 girls from 2 to eight.) It has served various purposes through the years, and in recent years, with no residents it has served as a storage area and home for the Auxiliary's flea market. Or Shedden Cottage, opened in 1911, it originally housed the crippled children of the Home (20 individuals). In later years it housed the older boys ranging in age from 11 to 17 years. Today it is home to staff members.
.

Just as the office and residential buildings were improved, in the early part of the 20th Century, so too was the farm improved and enlarged to meet the food demands of the resident population. By 1920 the Farm consisted of 165 acres of arable land on which were produced most of the food needs for the children and staff. The vegetable crop output included Irish potatoes, sweet potatoes, beans, peas, cabbage, onions, okra, and squash. Several acres were devoted to watermelons and cantaloupes. A peach orchard, a pecan grove, and a scuppernong grape arbor provided a welcome variety of edibles. Among the staple crops, 30-40 acres were planted annually to corn, oats and hay for animal fodder. By 1920 the farm had also acquired a grist mill (powered by the laundry boiler) enabling them to produce their own corn meal for baking breads for the Home

In addition to forage and row crops the farm also maintained various kinds of livestock including, in 1920, 4 mules, 49 hogs and pigs, numerous chickens, and a milking herd of 16 Jersey cows. Hogs were slaughtered on special occasions and when meat for seasoning was needed. The slaughter operation was a big event for the children both the boys who did the work and the girls who kibitzed the procedure (see Recollections Chapter).

As available living quarters had been expanded in the last decade of the 19th Century, so too had the number of resident orphans increased. The average year-end population of orphans had increase from 29 in the first five years to 119 by 1925 (See Table 1).

Table 1. UMCH Average Annual Orphan Population in First 55 Years by 5 Periods. Calculated From Year End Census Data.*

Years	Average Annual Population	Years	Average Annual Population
1871-1875	29	1901-1905	140
1876-1880	20	1906-1910	133
1881-1885	31	1911-1915	125
1886-1890	54	1916-1920	123
1891-1895	50	1921-1925	119
1896-1900	70	.	

* Calculations include several individual years in which population is estimated.

Certain characteristics of the orphan population are informative. Using the data for 1920 as representative, the age and sex distribution of the orphan population is shown in Table 2.

Table 2. Age-Sex Distribution of Orphans for Year 1920

Sex	Under 6 years	Age 6-9	9-12	12-15	over 15
Boys	5	9	16	24	8
Girls	3	8	5	23	23

Of these 124 children, 40 were full orphans (no living parent), 45 had a single living parent available, and 39 had both parents living. The higher retention of older girls in contrast to the loss of older boys was typical of the time. It was easy for teenage boys to get good paying jobs. This was not the case for teenage girls and they tended to stay in the Home longer. Girls were, for the most part, expected to remain in the Home (or family residence if not institutionalized) until they married or became middle aged. This, after all, was before women's emancipation, before they got the vote, and before NOW, ERA etc.

The health of the children was at all times a major concern for the administration. In a confined institutional environment where contagious diseases are known to spread rapidly and with a population of young children constantly exposed to one another and to outsiders, there was the ever-present risk that some infection would run through the population. Surprisingly, there were remarkably few such problems. One outbreak of diphtheria was mentioned but no deaths were noted. Even in the great worldwide influenza pandemic of 1917-1918, which killed more people than any disease outbreak in the history of mankind, there were no serious respiratory illnesses and no influenza deaths at the Home.

There was no infirmary on the campus in those days. In the case of "normal" pediatric infectious disease such as measles, mumps, or chicken pox, ill children were confined to their residence cottages but no effort was made to isolate the sick children from healthy children in the cottage. It was a common belief (with some justification) that early exposure to childhood diseases was less likely to be accompanied by serious complications than exposure at a later age.

A physician regularly visited the Home to check on the health of the children and to administer routine immunizations. (All children were immunized against smallpox and typhoid fever.) Should one be needed, a physician was available on call from Decatur. Should a serious emergency arise, children were taken to the hospital in Decatur.

Dental care was provided by volunteer dentists from Decatur who visited regularly and provided the necessary dental treatment.

In its first 25 years there had been only one resident orphan death at the Home. This changed early in the 20th century both because the resident population was now several times greater than it had been in earlier decades, and because the Home had gradually adopted a policy of accepting any applicant regardless of age or health status, something it had not been willing to do in the earliest years of limited resources. As noted in the trustees report of 1905, the Home stood ready to accept "all who needed its benefits"...including "babes of only a few weeks old, the crippled and the feeble-minded." Interestingly, while the state government had provisions to assist in care of most orphaned and abandoned children, it offered no protection or support for what were described as the "feeble-minded". Sadly, in 1903 two children died in the Home. One was a paralyzed child and the other a "feeble-minded" youngster. The specific illnesses of the two children and the causes of their deaths were not identified as was typical of the period given the primitive state of contemporary diagnostic medicine. It is not clear what happened to the remains of these two, but commonly in later years children dying on the campus were interred in the nearby Decatur Cemetery, and it seems probable that this was the case here.

Decatur Cemetery showing plots 67 and 68 where many children from the Home were buried in early years.

Little evidence remains today in the Decatur Cemetery of children from the Home who are buried there. There are two contiguous plots (numbers 67 and 68) and another separate plot (number 10) which contain the remains of about 31 children. Their names are listed in the cemetery office and a few names are still legible on the tiny headstones but for the most part that is all.

Mortality among the orphans was not considered excessive and, in fact, the Home was regularly commended for having an excellent health record, comparing favorably with any other institution or the general public environment. Table 3 shows mortality rates at the Home in the first years of the 20th century.

Table 3. Average Orphan Population and Actual Mortality by 5 Year Periods In First Quarter of the Twentieth Century

	1901-05	1906-10	1911-15	1916-20	1920-25
Population *	140	133	125	123	119
Deaths **	6	3	6	3	1

* At the end of reporting year as stated in trustees annual report.
** Of the 19 deaths occurring between 1901 and 1925, one was an accidental drowning, two were probably due to congenital defects, and the remaining 16 were probably infectious diseases, especially tuberculosis.

The Home 's policy for admission, as noted earlier, had been very lax in earlier years but was strengthened towards the end of this period such that children were accepted only between the ages of one and 12 years (exceptions were made); parents or other responsible adults were required to sign a release agreeing to relinquish any and all claims on the child admitted; and a medical examination was required prior to acceptance of any child to ensure that he or she had no major infectious illnesses, especially tuberculosis or venereal disease, two of the major scourges of the day.

A large farm bell mounted on a twelve foot wooden pedestal played a big role in the life of the children and is remembered, even today, by former residents of forty years ago for its importance in their lives. The bell had been purchased by Mr.

Asa G. Candler (of Coca-Cola fame) shortly after the Civil War for use in the Methodist Church in Villa Rica, Georgia. When the Villa Rica church was razed some years later, Mr. Candler repurchased it and donated it to the orphanage. The bell was used much as one might use a bugle on a military installation, to signal the time for certain events. It was rung at 6:30AM to

Farm bell used in early years to summon children to meals or other special events.

awaken the children and again at 7:00 am to call them to breakfast. Actually it was rung twice for each meal. It was rung first to tell the children to "stop whatever they were doing, get cleaned up, and get ready for mealtime", and second to tell them to "come and get it". At the second bell the children met outside and "queued up" by their cottages and marched to the dining hall. Children from a given cottage ate together. All stood by their chairs until the blessing had been offered and the dinner bell (a hand bell held by the superintendent or other official) had been rung and they then sat down to eat. Meals were served family style with each child helping him or herself except that the very small children were served on trays by the older girls. After the meal the older girls cleared the tables and washed and dried the dishes.

The aforementioned bell played another role during its active span at the Home. During World War II it served as a warning system in event of potential air raids. One resident (Bob Bell) remembers with some detail his unique responsibility during the war years. If enemy aircraft had been reported in the area he was to go to the bell and when he sighted the incoming aircraft he was to ring the bell loudly and continuously to warn the children to seek protection in their assigned shelter areas.

The quality of food might not seem like much by today's dietary standards but by contemporary measures it was deemed adequate and did not seem to cause any problems, at least not at this Home, though in some other contemporary orphanages pellagra (niacin deficiency) was a problem at times. Breakfast usually consisted of some combination of cereal, milk, bread and syrup, eggs, rice and gravy. Dinner (lunch), the big meal of the day, was vegetables and fruits in season grown on the farm, meat three times a week, and dessert twice a week in winter and ice cream almost daily in summer. Supper was a light meal of soup or rice and gravy, milk, bread and butter.

After meals the children were dismissed and returned to their cottages unsupervised or were free for a period of time until the next activity i.e. school or work.

Given the ever-changing character of the orphan population at the Home, the individual proclivities of the various superintendents and their staffs, and the impact of changing external influences, it would be impossible to identify any one point in time and describe it as "typical" of life in the Home for the 125 years of its existence. It seems, however, appropriate to select for examination a period during which Home life could be considered consistent in most respects, with that which was nearest the "typical" life. The early 20th century (i.e.1910 to 1920) arguably comes as close to representing "typical" life as any time. While many of the modern conveniences we accept today as essential were not in use in the Home at that time, neither were they in general use in the normal population. Also, the Home, reflecting contemporary society, was more agrarian oriented than modern society. Where the Home produced much of its own food, today that is inconceivable, but in the early 20th century it was not an unusual situation.

Life in Atlanta Cottage was as typical as in any other of the cottages of the day. Built in 1906 Atlanta Cottage was equipped with all the modern features. It was built of stone (as noted earlier, for fire protection), two stories high with front and rear covered porches, in the classic, plain, "boxy" style of the time, nothing ornate about it. In the 1920s it was home for 24 older girls from 14 to 20, and 10 or more babies from 2 to 8.

In the 1910-1920 period both the elementary (secondary) and high school education were provided on the campus just as they had been since the beginning. Three school rooms were located on the second floor of the Hawkins building. The school term was identical to that followed by the "in town" schools, nine months duration from September to June. However, school at the Home was taught in two sessions, one group going from 7:30 a.m. in the morning until 11:30 a.m. and the second "shift" going from twelve noon until 4:00 p.m. The half of the day not devoted to school, the children spent working at the Home- on the farm for the boys and household work for the girls. Only the very young were exempted from work. Jobs were available for all other ages. Girls who were so inclined were also given music lessons and some became accomplished musicians.

On completion of high school, boys and girls who demonstrated ability and wished to continue their education were given the option of going on to college at Home expense. Girls could attend LaGrange Junior College, Wesleyan College, or Young Harris College. Boys could go to Young Harris or Emory College. There was also an option for limited vocational training if the student preferred that. Boys got training in agriculture, which was really a continuation and extension of the farm training they got working at the Home. Girls got what today would be called "home economics". Like the boys this consisted of further experience in what they did at the Home - cooking, sewing, home care etc. They also got additional experience in dairy manufacture, *i.e.* butter and ice cream production.

50

During the one-half day the children were not in school, they were required to work at the Home. The boys worked primarily on the farm under supervision of the farm manager who usually had one or two farm laborer employees in addition to the boys. The children did almost all of the farm work, plowing, caring for the animals, milking, planting row crops and harvesting crops. The farm manager, as supervisor, established the program for the farm production, determined what work needed to be done, what crops would be planted and when harvested. The boys, as they gained experience, were allowed to play a larger role in decision making and determining what needed to be done when. Similarly, the girls were occupied in housekeeping chores, preparing and serving food, cleaning after meals, doing the laundry, sewing, etc.

The necessity of working communally for the welfare of all, and with limited direct supervision, tended to make both boys and girls somewhat independent and responsible persons at an early age. However, this same independence which developed early in the Home children had a negative side as well. In the early 1900s, particularly between 1917 and 1920, many young boys feeling "able to make it on their own" ran away from the Home seeking an independent life. This was in part due to the unusual demand for labor during and after the war and the great expansion of industry which created a huge need for skilled and unskilled labor. This craving for independence was also reflected in young men from the Home volunteering as soldiers during World War I. No data are available on how many Home children went to war, but an August 1918 report notes that one Home soldier was wounded in battle and a later report notes his death as the first among Home soldiers. In 1919 Superintendent Hawkins reported that of the 23 residents who went to war that year, none had been killed. When hard times hit the country in later years and fewer jobs were available and low wages became the norm, this spate of early "unscheduled" departures ceased.

At the Home all was not just school and work. There was ample time for play. In the cottages housing the smaller children there was always a playroom well equipped with toys and often sandboxes in which to play during "free time". Weather permitting most children played out of doors during daylight hours. Marbles were a favorite game of both boys and girls. The usual "hide and seek" games were a common form of recreation. For older children there was a tennis court which, weather permitting, stayed fully occupied during play hours. Children also were allowed to produce plays and other staged activities for the Home audience. Often they were helped and guided in these stage activities by students from Agnes Scott College or other outside groups.

During this "typical" period of home life as described above, the Reverend J.M. Hawkins was superintendent, his wife was matron, and their daughter was assistant matron. Two additional matrons were employed during the nine months' school year but were replaced by older resident girls during the summer months. A Professor M.T. Parker was employed as principal of the campus school and Mr. Hawkins' son was assistant teacher. There was also a farm superintendent and his assistant, and two cooks.

~ 6 ~

The 20ᵗʰ Century, Second Quarter (1926-1950)

The second quarter of the century was characterized by continuation of the growth and prosperity of the previous quarter. The two major events of this quarter, the Great Depression (1929-1939) and World War II (1941-1945) had limited impact on the Home. Though the Depression officially began with the stock market crash of October 1929 it took several years for the full impact to be felt throughout all walks of life across the United States.

By 1933 the Depression was in full swing throughout the country and many Methodist programs were feeling the effects of reduced income. However the Home was little impacted by this financial crisis; it remained free from debt and continued to pay its bills on time. This ability to remain solvent and unencumbered by debt was the result of several factors: the efficient management by the Reverend J.M. Hawkins and his wife, Matron Mamie Hawkins; the continued generosity of the North Georgia Conference congregations in spite of strained financial times; and the fact that the Home was, to a considerable extent, self-sufficient, producing most of the food consumed at the Home. Annual income and expenditures at the Home declined somewhat during the peak years of the Depression but never to the point that any critical programs were threatened. In fact, it is doubtful that the children were even aware of any financial crisis except as they most certainly must have heard of it through the news media (radio or newspaper) or from their non-institutional classmates at school.

Not fully appreciated by many observers of the Home was the importance of the roles played by the three most critical employees of the orphanage - the superintendent, the matron (his wife), and the agent. The Home had been blessed with a series of competent and effective leaders since its beginning, without exception. In the early 20th century the Reverend C.A. Jamison had done an outstanding job as superintendent since 1903, but was compelled to resign after his wife had to give up the matronship. Tending to the needs of over 100 children had left Mrs. Jamison totally exhausted and she resigned in mid-year of 1909. Because of her poor health, he resigned in October of the same year. Fortunately for the Home, Agent Crumley remained on the job through the transition to a new superintendent and matron. Following the Jamisons, Reverend J. M. Hawkins and his wife were appointed superintendent and matron respectively.

The Hawkins worked at the Home for 27 years (he served three years as Superintendent and 24 years as Agent/Superintendent), and she as Senior Matron throughout his tenure. Both were highly regarded by the Trustees, the staff at the Home, and the children - to whom he was "Uncle Mat and she was Aunt Mamie". Dr. Hawkins' ill health forced them to resign in 1933 to the sorrow of all concerned. However, his influence continued for several years after his departure since the next Superintendent was Dr. Ralph Hawkins, his son, who was appointed after his father resigned and who espoused the same philosophy as had his father.

In 1934, the Depression notwithstanding, the churches and Missionary Societies of the North Georgia Conference were generous in their support of the Home. Their donations made it possible to make extensive repairs and renovations to the interior of several of the cottages which were by now showing the wear of years of young residents. Over the next three years more improvements were made to the facility. A large new feed barn was erected to meet the needs of the growing dairy operation.

54

Plumbing and electrical fixtures were repaired, replaced, or installed for the first time. (One might remember that the thirties were the years that indoor plumbing and electricity were installed in many homes throughout the country for the first time.)

In 1934 a seemingly minor name change was made that acknowledged the changing direction being taken with regard to admittance policies. The Orphanage became the Methodist Children's Home. Increasingly children were being accepted by the Home who were not true orphans, but were children in need of a stable home. Oft times, the parents had fallen onto bad times and simply could not afford to care for their offspring. The Home provided a recourse, sometimes a temporary one as the children could be retrieved by the parents if they became able to care for them again.

At the end of 1933 there were 67 children in residence, and in 1934 there were 80. In 1936 there were 112, almost twice the number of only three years earlier. This was a direct consequence of the Depression as jobless and destitute families found themselves unable to cope with the financial burden of raising a family and were forced to relinquish their children to institutions as a better alternative to abandoning them to the streets.

In 1936, Dr. Ralph Hawkins, who had served as Agent/Superintendent for the preceding three years, resigned in order to return to the pastorate which he loved, and the Reverend Fred L. Glisson was appointed to replace him. As had become standard policy, his wife joined the staff at the same time as Senior Matron. Improving education was a particular goal of the Glissons and by 1936 the elementary school (grades 1 to 7) on campus employed three full-time teachers and was considered equal to any local public school. At this time, two older children attended Decatur High School and eight others were at Avondale High School. One older child was attending Young Harris College. Expenses for the college student were donated by one of the Trustees since no clear policy dictated that the Home would provide funds for college education (though they always seemed to find the money when needed.)

Superintendent Fred Glisson and several Home staff members having fun. About 1943

In 1937 there were 115 children in the Home. Attending staff had grown along with the children's numbers and there were now, in addition to the Glissons, 16 assistants helping with one part or another of the Home's operation. Many improvements were made during this period in the physical facility, mostly repairing buildings that had begun to deteriorate with age. Clearly much still remained to be done since an inspection that year confirmed that not one of the cottages met the state's current standards. A most critical need according to the Trustees (and presumably the state) was an infirmary where sick children could receive proper medical care and be isolated from the general Home population. This is not to say that the children received inadequate medical care- they did not. The combined resources of the DeKalb County Health Department and the volunteer local physicians and dentists gave the Home children as good medical care as they could have hoped for on the "outside". Along with other health concerns at this time, good nutrition had become recognized as important. To ensure an adequate diet for the children, a dietitian (Mrs. R. H. Gonzales) was now hired to

56

design menus and supervise preparation of meals that would provide the children with balanced healthy meals.

In 1937 and 1938 many more Home improvements were completed. Cottages were remodeled and refurbished to make them more comfortable and more appealing. Fire escapes were installed in all residential cottages as required by the state. More bathrooms were installed in some of the cottages. Plumbing and electrical utilities were further improved over what had already been done in the past several years. For the farm, another new barn and a garage were erected. In 1938 and 1939 new refrigeration systems were installed in the main kitchen and the dairy.

Another change about this time resulted from the determination of one Thomas Penland, an insurance agent in Decatur. Penland was (during 1935-1938) President of the Atlanta Methodist Young People's Union, a group representing about 50 Atlanta Methodist churches (later renamed the Epworth League). One member of the Union was Kathleen Glisson, daughter of Superintendent Fred Glisson. She told the members that the Home had a real need for a bus to transport the children back and forth to school, special events etc. Penland was impressed that the need was valid and set about to raise the necessary funds through the AMYPU. He caused to be issued shares of stock known as "Shares of Happiness" at a cost of $1.00/ share with all monies collected committed to the purchase of a vehicle for the Home. Through this mechanism he raised $1800.00 and purchased a yellow school bus which was presented to the Home on Christmas Day 1937. Everyone at the Home and in the AMYPU was so pleased with the project that the following year it was repeated and a second vehicle was purchased. For whatever reason the yellow <u>Happiness Bus</u> (as it came to be called) has become an icon of the Home and at annual reunions one still sees a model of the yellow bus on display in some prominent spot, though the busses themselves have given way to modern day vans.

Again reflecting the Glissons passion for education, more effort was directed at schooling. For the first time serious effort was made to develop both music and athletic programs. A new grand piano was purchased and lessons were offered to those students who wanted them and exhibited some musical aptitude.

By the end of 1938 there were 139 children living at the Home. Financially the Home was doing very well, the Depression notwithstanding. Work Day in 1938 brought in $13,000.00. And again, all bills were paid promptly and fully, this in spite of the fact that operating expenses were now averaging $100.00 a day.

This year the Board of Trustees was increased to 19 members; the expansion was felt necessary to effectively conduct the ever-increasing business of the Home. The board continued to meet quarterly as it had in the past. Growth of the Home continued into the next year belying any threats from the Depression. In 1939 the Joseph P. Whitehead Foundation - a long time supporter of the Home - provided funds for the erection of a modern school building on campus to be used as a grammar school (grades 1 through 7) and known as the Joseph P. Whitehead School.

Each year more modifications, improvements, and additions were made as the needs of the Home grew. By 1940 new heating units had been added to each cottage (at a cost of $5000.00, but to the great relief of cottage residents in the winter months.) A new workshop was also added for use by maintenance personnel and the older boys. (This was not a recreational addition although the boys greatly enjoyed working there. They manufactured much of the furniture used in the cottages including beds, chairs, etc.). For the girls, new laundry machines were purchased and most importantly for all, a six-inch water line was installed from the Decatur Water Works to the Home. Its installation ended the need for two separate water systems as had been used for years - one for cooking and drinking (from Decatur Water Works) and a separate one for bathing, cleaning and farm use with this water coming from the Home's well. Also in 1940 the building of the infirmary was begun. At the end of this year there were 136 children in residency.

In 1940 Dr. Frank Quillian replaced Dr. Glisson as Superintendent but served in that role for only one year. He continued, however to serve the Home many years in other capacities.

In 1941 the Joseph P. Whitehead Foundation, which had only recently funded the new school on campus, now donated an additional $15000.00 to be used for various and sundry repairs which included refurbishing several cottages, replacement of outdated kitchen equipment, new farm equipment, and other upgrades for the buildings. This same year, Mr. H. B. Mays took over as Superintendent and served in that role for most of the war years (1941-1944). He was the first lay Superintendent in the history of the Home.

Also, in the early 1940s an experiment (later to become standard policy) was tried for the first time whereby a dining room and kitchen were installed in the older girl's cottage. The justification for this change was the judgment of the board and the administrators that preparing and serving meals and eating in the individual cottages was more "home-like" than the institutional practice of cooking and eating *en masse* in the large dining hall. In addition to providing a more home-like environment than that in the large dining hall with its cafeteria style eating, it gave the girls -at least those in this cottage- experience with cooking and serving meals in a family setting. This first "cottage kitchen" was conceived and largely paid for by the First Methodist Church of Atlanta. How or why they devised this concept is not known but it was well received by all. The concept proved so successful that it eventually became the standard throughout all of the Home cottages.

The year 1941 was an active one for the Home. All of the children were sent for two weeks summer vacation to St. Simons Island off the south Georgia coast and by all accounts this trip

59

was a resounding success. Many of the children had never seen an ocean before and the trip remained a mealtime topic of conversation long after the summer had passed.

The Home's Boy Scout Troop and Girl Reserves were reorganized this summer and both became involved in more and different activities than they had been in the past. New volunteer leaders were a great help in making these groups more viable. With assistance from the WPA (Works Project Administration - a Roosevelt depression program created to provide jobs for thousands of the unemployed) night classes in typing and shorthand were started. This training was designed to prepare the older girls for becoming financially self-supporting when they entered the outside world. Additionally, art classes were organized and run by church volunteers, not to improve their earning abilities, but to expose the children to cultural activities they might otherwise miss in the Home life.

Atlanta Cottage Girls 1947

Atlanta Cottage girls having a party, probably someone's birthday.
1953

UMCH Boy Scout Troop 9. 1940

Bench made by Home scouts for use in the Home. 1941

By 1942 the World War was beginning to be felt at the Home though not in a particularly negative way. One 18 year old "graduate" of the Home had joined the Army and been trained as a radio operator. (What became of him is unclear.) Several other boys had secured well paying jobs in the coastal cities of Savannah and Mobile where they worked as welders in shipyards which were going "full-tilt" trying to build ships to meet the war's needs. Over the next three years over a dozen young men joined the military to serve their country. One became a lieutenant in the Army Air Force and served as a B-17 bomber pilot in the European theater. After completing 25 missions over Germany without injury he was rotated back to the states (standard procedure). Another "Home boy" served as a lieutenant in the Coast Guard. Several landed with their Army units in Normandy on D-Day; two more served in the Pacific Theater where they saw action in the Okinawa campaign. Before the war was over, some 20 young men from the Home were serving in the military. At least two of them were cited for bravery and one was awarded the Distinguished Flying Cross with three oak leaf clusters. So far as is known, none of the Home's military men were wounded or killed during the war.

Several girls got jobs in government offices and private companies - in some cases replacing men who had been called into the military. At least one girl trained and served as a Navy nurse, though her actual wartime duty assignments are not recorded.

At the Home, members of the Boy Scout Troop assumed the role of Air Raid Wardens on campus. In event of an air raid or other disaster it was their responsibility to gather up the smaller children and herd them to a designated safe shelter. Unlike wardens in some other areas, these scouts apparently were not responsible for ensuring that blackout curtains had been properly closed or that fire control equipment was appropriately distributed. Meanwhile, at the Home's woodworking shop, older boys designed and manufactured electric food evaporators which were sold to homeowners to be used to preserve excess victory garden produce in keeping with the government's request that everyone conserve food in behalf of the war effort. The monies collected from their sale went to help cover Home expenses.

Not only the children were involved. During these years some 13 staff members completed the Red Cross Standard First Aid Course to help prepare them to cope with any emergency that might arise.

Otherwise, life at the Home continued little affected by the war. One noticeable impact was the enthusiastic patriotism exhibited by the children, especially as it related to military activities involving former residents. Any activity in which their alumnae participated was followed with great enthusiasm and pride and a visit back to the Home by a military alumnus on leave was cause for much flag waving celebration.

In 1942 a new cottage was erected for older boys (Smith cottage), again like the new girl's cottage, paid for largely by the Whitehead Foundation. Other cottages were repaired and refurbished as the need and resources allowed. The new infirmary was furnished with beds and medical equipment providing four separate wards with accommodations for a total

63

of 18 patients. Its opening was cause for much thankfulness, especially in light of the tragic polio outbreak which had occurred the previous year. The infirmary was staffed with a part-time nurse and served by volunteer physicians, dentists, and nurses from Decatur medical facilities as required.

A new sewage system serving the entire lower part of the campus (the farm area) was installed this year.

Recreation and entertainment were not slighted during the war years. In 1942 the children were again treated to a two-week vacation at Camp Rutledge and during the year they were admitted free to visiting entertainments including the Southeastern Fair and the Ringling Brothers circus. In season, Easter egg hunts, outdoor picnics, and Christmas parties were part of their recreational program.

At the Home, the new infirmary saw some use as an outpatient facility but otherwise remained under utilized - to the management's delight. Credit here goes to Dr. W. P. Smith, medical director, and to his graduate nurse assistant who was now a full time employee. These two saw to the needs of the children and were ever alert to recognizing and controlling any outbreak of infectious disease before it could erupt throughout the campus. There were several cases of mumps in the Spring of 1943 that required hospitalization in the infirmary, but little else.

For recreation the children now had a new pool which was widely used in warm weather. This year a Girl Reserve Group was organized in the Williams Cottage and a Blue Bird Group in the Epworth Cottage for the younger girls. Walton Cottage was home to an active Girl Scout Troop. The boys continued to actively participate in the Boy Scout Troop. Holidays continued to be celebrated as major activities throughout the year with significant support provided by local volunteer groups. For Easter, there were Easter egg hunts, wiener roasts, and parties. Individual children were selected and sponsored by different churches and Sunday School classes. Christmas in 1943 was celebrated with a turkey feast donated by the Marietta First

Methodist Church. Dinner was followed by distribution of two truckloads of toys donated by Sears Roebuck Company, and a load of fresh fruit which was contributed by the State Farmer's Market. Later the children were treated to the Barnum and Bailey Circus and the Shrine Circus. Throughout the year local theatre managers donated tickets to permit each child to attend one movie each week, with some discretion used in determining which movies the children were allowed to attend. This weekly movie became a treasured outing for most of the children as they went in groups with the older ones serving as chaperones for the youngest.

Perhaps this is an appropriate time to make special mention of some of the groups that have consistently aided the Home and made life for the children more enjoyable. As noted several times already, the Joseph P. Whitehead Foundation has been a most frequent and generous contributor to the Home, being responsible for funding several of the buildings on campus and financing numerous other support programs through the years. The Whitehead Foundation was, and is, one of the charitable organizations funded directly or indirectly by the Coca Cola Company or its officers. The Warner Hill Bible Class of the St. Mark Church had, and continued to make it possible for the children to attend summer camp each year as well as to attend various entertainment activities through the year. The Women's Auxiliary has been a committed support group that did much for the Home - as it continues to do so today.

The immediate post-war years were a time for readjustment throughout the country. As military personnel returned home there were numerous instances of family discord as husbands and wives found they had become incompatible during the years of separation. This increase in family dysfunction caused a temporary increase in applications and admission of children to the Home.

Life soon returned to normal across the country and business activity boomed. Manufacturers rushed to catch up on making cars, machinery, and equipment that had been stopped because

65

of material shortages and military priorities during the war; construction of homes grew at an unprecedented pace; in every quarter growth and expansion were setting new records. This flurry of activity created jobs galore and that in turn had impact on the Home as young men and women were quick to leave the Home and seek employment in the expanding economy where they could make unheard of salaries.

In 1945 Reverend B. C. Kerr was appointed Superintendent and began what would be one of the longer and more productive and memorable tenures, or at least so it appears to this author. Perhaps that assessment is influenced by the fact that most of the former residents interviewed in developing this history were living on campus at some time during Mr. Kerr's tenure and seem to remember him most fondly and enjoy recalling events with which he was associated.

A brief biographical sketch may be appropriate. Bramwell C. Kerr was born May 7th, 1896 in Metcalf, Georgia, the son of a Methodist preacher. He attended Emory University and studied for the ministry, was ordained a Methodist minister, and pastored churches in Atlanta, Athens, LaGrange, and Loganville, Georgia. He then joined the Children's Home where he served as Superintendent from 1944 to 1960. His wife, Katie Mae Bennett (Kerr) worked with him at the Home and was similarly beloved by the children. They retired from the Home in 1960, and he passed away in July 1986.

At the Home, life resumed its normal pace as wartime activities were replaced with more conventional activities. Schooling continued as a major interest of Superintendent Kerr as it had been of his predecessor. By 1945 there were four teachers employed full-time at the Home school. In addition to normal educational pursuits (the Home school maintained its high standing among community schools), special attention was given to providing musical training for those individuals who exhibited an aptitude for music. Through the programs of the Boy Scouts and Camp Fire Girls, children received training in non-academic pursuits such as woodworking, handicrafts, and homemaking. By the end of 1945 five girls were away at college, two at LaGrange, one at Andrew, one at Toccoa Falls Institute, and one at Reinhardt College.

On campus many much-needed repairs were made. The Shedden cottage, worn from years of use and abuse was completely restored. All other cottages were repaired and painted as necessary to bring them up to acceptable standards as had been impossible during the war years. In anticipation of a sizable donation from the Whitehead Foundation the following year, plans were drawn up for a new recreations center complete with swimming pool and gym (later replaced by a new and modern gym in 1960) and for the complete renovation of the main kitchen including replacement of outdated refrigeration equipment.

In keeping with the fast pace of growth throughout the country at this time, donations reached new highs in the late 1940s. In 1945 the annual Work Day donations totalled over $54,000, and in 1946 it exceeded $60,000. At the same time generous gifts were received from several individual donors.

Four lads from Home camping out on campus grounds. About 1946

The year 1946 was a "Red Letter Year" as the Home celebrated its 75th Anniversary on the 29th of September. Celebratory exercises were held in the Whitehead School auditorium beginning at 2:30 in the afternoon. In addition to most present and many former trustees and superintendents of the Home the celebration was attended by city and county dignitaries as well as numerous alumnae of the Home. Following the formal program, the children led a processional to the grave of founder Jesse Boring where they placed flowers about the headstone in memory of the one who was single handedly responsible for establishment of the Home.

This same year, perhaps in honor of its 75th anniversary, the Home initiated publication of *Pen Points*, a quarterly newsletter describing personalities and ongoing activities at the Home. This publication would thrive and entertain and educate friends of the Home for the next several years, eventually to be replaced by the current bimonthly newsletter, *Signposts.*

An interesting event occurred in 1946, interesting because it shows how times have changed in the subsequent 50 plus years, and changed for the better. It would be disturbing but for the fact that the episode illustrates a philosophy of prejudice that existed in the 1940s but has since largely disappeared. In 1946 three half-Chinese children, (their father was born in America and their mother was a native Chinese) were proposed for admission to the Home. Their father, who fought in World War I, had married a Chinese girl who returned with him to the states where the two worked in the laundry business and enjoyed a good reputation for honesty and industriousness. Both parents died leaving the children with no identifiable relatives or means of support in this country.   Reacting to the children's plight, their church pastor, Reverend Hoke Sewell appealed to the UMCH for help. However, before he would accept them into the Home, the then superintendent, Mr. Kerr, felt it necessary to poll the resident children to see if they would object to having a family of "Chinese" children as members of their extended family. Without exception the resident children approved the idea and the Asian children were accepted. The idea of having to seek approval for inclusion of minority children would be anathema today, but in the 1940s it seemed appropriate. The decision turned out to be a good one in many ways, The Chinese children proved to be exceptionally good students, well motivated, and outstanding members of the UMCH community. They later went on to successful careers all the while remaining loyal to their roots at the Home. Two of these children were in attendance at the 1998 UMCH reunion in Macon, Georgia, and the reaction of fellow "brothers and sisters" showed that they were still highly regarded as outstanding members of the "big family".

In this and the following several years, the Home was flooded with requests for child placement, the increase largely a response to family disruptions resulting from the war. Pleas for admission were literally received almost every day but unfortunately the Home was full and there was no way many of the requests could be honored. Plans were drawn up for erection of a new cottage and modernization and expansion of the central kitchen but work was delayed by the shortage of available building materials in this booming post-war period.

The farm had suffered badly during the war years. Feed, seed, building materials, and farm equipment had been almost unattainable for several years but as these items came available, the newly appointed farm manager, a Mr. Lanier, graduate of the agricultural department at the University of Georgia, did an excellent job of rejuvenating the farm and turning it into a profitable operation again. By 1949 the dairy was producing upwards of 45 gallons of milk a day, most of the vegetables, and some of the meats consumed at the Home. As a result of this return to high production, plans were developed for construction of a cannery to enable the Home to preserve that food which could not be consumed as it was produced. Not surprisingly, the Whitehead Foundation contributed the monies for the cannery.

For those children fortunate enough to be in the Home, life was good. The children's health, though a matter of constant concern, remained remarkably good. Some have attributed this to the addition of a dietitian on campus who ensured balanced quality meals. Others credited the availability of top quality medical help. During this year the health of the children received particular attention and medical and dental care were provided on a regular basis for prevention of illness and at any time for emergency needs. Two children underwent major surgery in 1949 and both recovered uneventfully. The dentist visited every week and ensured the development of fine teeth for the children.

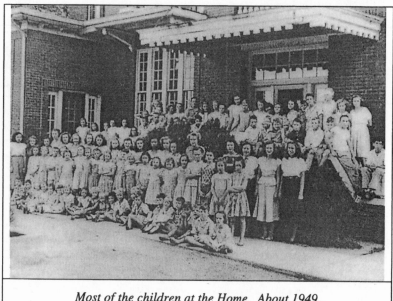

Most of the children at the Home. About 1949

The infirmary was happily under utilized. Not until 1949 had there been any significant illness since the two surgical cases in 1943. Just after Christmas in 1949 a number of children became sick with an unknown illness. It was called virus X disease, so called because it came on suddenly, did not resemble any common pediatric disease, and it appeared to be something new and different. During this outbreak a number of children were confined to the infirmary which gave that facility a good "shake down" and also helped justify its existence to any who might have questioned its value. After several days' illness all patients recovered almost as mysteriously as they had become ill.

Certainly the excellent medical care provided by Dr. J. E. Leslie, Decatur physician, and Mrs. Sam Dunlap the resident nurse, were important factors in the speedy recovery of all of the children and with no residual after effects.

Again, recreational needs were well satisfied. Thanks to the Warner Hill Bible Class, the Women's Auxiliary, the Decatur Lion's Club, and numerous Sunday School Classes and other church and civic groups, the children went to summer camp in 1947 at Camp Optimist, Lakemont, attended the Shrine Circus, and partook of many other local area events.

Financially the Home was doing remarkably well. Work Day had produced some $60,000 dollars, churches and Sunday Schools were unusually generous, and bequests were beginning to mount up.

~ 7 ~

Modern Times, The Golden Years
1951-1965

The fifteen years beginning in 1951 might well be called the "golden years" of the Home. The Home's finances were no longer an uncertain issue; monies were available to meet all needs, thanks to the work of many. Following the examples set by earlier agents and supervisors, especially Sam Jones, Howard Crumley, and J. M. Hawkins, recent agents, supervisors, and administrators as B.C. Kerr, John Moore, and most recently (and still current) Beverly Cochran, implemented programs to provide for the financial needs of the Home and also to keep the Home up to date in meeting the needs of the children and the community it serves, whether it be providing adequate housing and support, or implementing changes in policy that better serve current needs. One major change in meeting financial requirements has been the increasing acceptance and reliance upon government funds as noted elsewhere in this text.

Through the 1950s and '60s the resident population varied but held at around 100 to 150 children, about the maximum that could be housed comfortably in the residence cottages. The resident population at the end of 1951 was 150 children. In 1962 the Georgia Department of Family and Children's Services (DFACS) stated that under then current policy the capacity for the Home was 150 children. In 1963 there were actually 151 children in residence. A look at Appendix E shows how the population has fluctuated and how it peaked in the mid-1950s and '60s.

In the 1950s major changes were made in schooling for the children. It was decided that it was no longer practical to hold classes on the campus and in fact it would be beneficial for the children's development to send them to school in town and so by 1951 all on campus schooling was terminated and the children were sent by bus to public schools in DeKalb County. They were distributed to four area schools with no more than five Home children in any one class, at least in the younger classes. Justified or not, there was concern that too many Home children in any one class might overwhelm the other students in the class. These concerns appear to have been valid (I suspect this was another manifestation of the extreme loyalty and camaraderie shared among the Home children which the other children found difficult to contend with). Home children did well in the new school environments, both academically and athletically. They frequently outshone the regular students in both areas, both in elementary and high schools. Older children attended several of the state colleges including LaGrange, Wesleyan, Young Harris, Abraham Baldwin, Emory at Oxford, West Georgia, Reinhardt and Asbury Colleges. On campus, The Whitehead Building, which had formerly served as the school was now converted to a children's residence cottage.

On campus, expansion of physical facilities was continuing at a rapid rate during this time. Leigh Cottage, named for Miss Leila Leigh of Newnan, Georgia, had been completed in 1949 and provided housing for the smallest children. Edwards Cottage, completed the following year was given in memory of Estelle Edwards Watkins by her brother Edgar Watkins to provide housing for older boys, and in 1955 another new cottage was added, Glenn Cottage, to house small children. It was designed to hold eighteen young girls, ages eight to eleven. It was built primarily with funds provided by the Glenn Memorial Methodist Church of Atlanta. Another building, the activities building or gymnasium, was made a special project and in 1965 this building along with an adjacent swimming pool, and tennis court and ball field was completed at a cost of $167,000.

In 1955 it was decided by the trustees that the Home had grown to the point that additional staff support was needed to serve the administrative needs of the Home and a new position, Assistant Supervisor and Business Manager was created. Mr. Harold Lanier was the first appointee to this position.

Religious training was not neglected in the 1950s. About two-thirds of the children regularly attended Pattillo Memorial Methodist Church in Decatur and the rest attended Decatur First Methodist. Apropos the earlier comment about problems when there were too many Home children in one class, it was eventually decided to stop accepting the Home children in Decatur First Sunday School classes as they reportedly outnumbered and overwhelmed the other students in the classes.

Health care, always a concern at the Home, was maintained at its usual high level during these years. With former superintendent Fred Glisson, now Director of Emory Hospital's Golden Cross program, the children had access to Emory's excellent medical care at all times. Hardly a day passed without several children being treated at the Emory medical facility. Further, the nearby Ponce de Leon Infirmary was always available for treating any eye, ear, nose, and throat problems, and Dr. Freeman Simmons, who had been appointed the Home's physician, was on call day and night for any problem that might arise.

The Decatur farm continued to be a productive asset, both for producing foodstuffs to be eaten at the Home, and for teaching the children responsibility and the value of a good work ethic. In 1960 there were 100 head of purebred whiteface Hereford cattle, about 25 hogs, and approximately 1000 chickens (this latter varied with seasonal consumption of birds).

Most of the comments from former residents in Chapter 10, _Recollections,_ are based on life at the Home in the 1950s and describe life at the Home during this period so that little more is needed of this era.

Home boys working on UMCH farm

Old wagons once used to haul milk and produce from the farm up to the kitchen.

Abandoned dairy barn with lake in background.

Farm tractor used by Home boys.

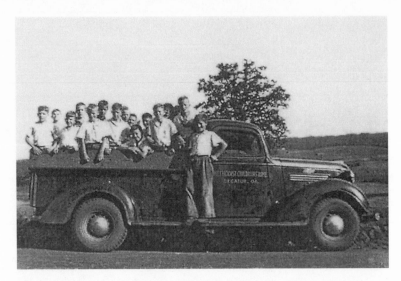

Truck load of Home boys.

Robert Mote milking cows in dairy barn. About 1954

Musical talent at work on the piano. About 1947

Charles Deal at controls of soap box derby entry. In the 1950s

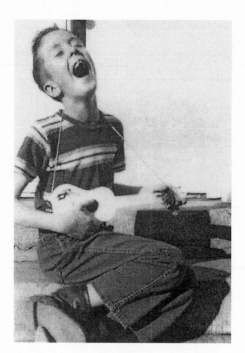

David Bailey entertaining with ukulele.
About 1953

UMCH Boy Scout Troop 9 preparing for trip to Silver Springs, Florida.
1954

The Home's pony, Major Doll, *and boys with Oscar Alton on top. 1946*

Christmas party in dining room. About 1946

Girls relaxing outdoors on a sunny summer day. About 1953

Girls playing in tree on campus. 1954

Home boys Robert Mote and Dan Lynch who drove the school bus.
About 1955

~ 8 ~

Changing Concepts

This Chapter and Chapter 14, *The Future*, are written with a somewhat different emphasis than the rest of the book. Chapters 8 and 14 are not directed exclusively to the UMCH in Decatur, Georgia. Instead they address general issues of *changing policies* and what these conceptual changes have meant and will mean to the Home. The issues discussed in these two chapters do relate to the Decatur UMCH but no more or less to children's homes all over the country, one no more than another.

In the early years of orphanages (the late 18th and early 19th centuries) the basis for their existence was relatively simple and uncomplicated - to provide a safe haven for orphaned or abandoned children where they might grow up to an age of self-sufficiency with a minimum of neglect and abuse. It was considered appropriate to provide adequate if minimal food, clothing, and shelter for the children and little else. Educational goals were top provide enough training to enable the "graduates" of a home to earn a living wage once they went out into the world; this usually meant training for employment in menial low-paying jobs. There was limited or no consideration given to social development of the children - how they might integrate with their peers on the "outside", their behavioral needs etc. A frequent and often valid complaint about orphanages of the time was that they were simply a place to park unwanted children while providing them with little help to prepare them for making it in the world after they were discharged from the orphanage.

The philosophy of providing minimal support for the dependent children prevailed through the 19th century, but beginning in the 20th century the quality of life care improved steadily in orphanages paralleling improvements in life outside the institutions and by the mid 20th century institutional life was not much different from life on the "outside". However, beginning slowly, as early as the 1930s, and rising to almost tidal wave proportions by the 1960s, major changes in children's homes philosophy occurred. No longer was "parking" children in an institution and providing them with minimum support deemed adequate. (Even though the limited support provided by institutions was usually far greater than that which the children had received before being placed in the institutional home.) By the end of the 1960s a whole new philosophy had evolved and resulted in major changes in how children's homes were operated. All sorts of new programs and policies had been installed; programs to help the children psychologically cope with their unfortunate status; programs to help dysfunctional families cope with parental responsibilities and enable them to accept their abandoned or abused children back into the home safely; policies which dictated how much an institution could require of the resident children; policies which defined how children could be disciplined by their home institution; programs and policies it seems almost *ad nauseum* all aimed at improving the lot of the children and all the while placing greater restrictions on the institution in one way or another.

How these new programs and their inherent controls were developed and why they were accepted is an example of how modern American government has assumed more and more responsibility in managing our individual lives.

In years past, support for orphanages almost always was provided by church groups and supplemented by donations from philanthropic individuals. However, during the Great Depression of the 1930s private support for many charitable programs was curtailed because institutions' and individuals' discretionary funds had been much reduced by the economic impact of the Depression. Into this financial crisis stepped the federal and state governments and provided support to replace that which was no longer available from the private sector. Without this government intervention many worthwhile charitable programs would have had to shut down for want of funds. However, along with providing financial support in this time of crisis, the government also assumed a regulatory role of untold proportions. How the government was able to acquire such an influential role in the management of private organizations is easily understood. In order to receive the government largesse - be it surplus food or money for capital improvements, or whatever, donees had to agree to accept government-developed guidelines for almost all aspects of their operation. Not many children's homes were able or willing to forego the financially attractive government support in order to remain independent and relatively free of governmental control. A few have. Government support and government guidelines are not necessarily bad in themselves. What happened however, was that those who were responsible for devising government guidelines under which homes must now operate often were (and are) not experienced in child care institution management and the new policies have not always been well designed to benefit the homes or the children.

In the 60 years since the Depression, government's role in the management of private institutions, of whatever type, and including children's homes, has continued to become more and more pervasive and more and more restrictive.

Some of the more significant changes in the past 30-40 years are identified here.

One of the major changes in child care concepts has been the development of new child placement recommendations, which minimize the use of institutional homes. It is widely agreed that returning the child to his/her biological family is the best solution fort he child IF the problem(s) which originally resulted in parent-child separation have been corrected. Too often today, with such strong pressure to return the child to biological parents, inadequate preassessment of parental capabilities has resulted in children being returned to an environment as bad as that from which they had been removed in the first place. The end result is that the child is likely to be abused as before, or worse, and then will have to be returned to the institution from which he/she had been outplaced.

The next best placement for children is usually considered to be the foster home. Again, as in the biological parent placement program, the concept is good but the reality is often not. With the pressure to use foster care (assuming biological parents are not available), children have frequently been placed (actually misplaced) in what turns out to be inappropriate foster homes. There are many reasons why a foster home may be the wrong choice for a child. Failure of officials to properly investigate the appropriateness of a given child-foster home placement is almost certain to result in the child being removed from that home and placed in another in hopes that the next home will provide a satisfactory child-family relationship. Because of inadequate preplacement evaluation, many times children are moved several times before (if ever) they find a suitable match of child and family which will develop the desired child-foster parent relationship. There are myriad horror stories of children being passed from home to home for five, six, seven or more times without a suitable environment ever being found. One recent Florida study showed that 29 percent of children in foster care in that state had been in five or more foster home placements. Children so passed around don't develop any family bonds and as such are less fortunate than institutionalized children who usually do develop bonds with their peers and/or with institutional staff persons at the home. This phenomenon of children moving through multiple foster care homes has become so common that the term "plastic bag brigade" has evolved to describe them because they often carry their belongings from home to home in plastic garbage bags.

Another reason for recommendations against institutional housing has been that institutions are accused of failing to provide the interpersonal relationship that is part of family in individual homes. To some extent this is true, but as pointed out, if foster home placement does not succeed and results in multiple moves, the institution is the better, more stable environment.

Costs of institutional management are often cited as militating against this type of housing. Indeed, institutional housing is more expensive than foster care or biological home care. One recent study has suggested that one child/year in foster care costs an average of $17,000, whereas one child/year in the institutional setting costs over $50,000. Even if this be correct, and it may not be in most instances, one must keep in mind the overall objective is to provide the child with the best possible environment in which to grow up, not the cheapest. Also, one factor which has raised institutional care costs is the restrictive governmental rules and regulations which now govern use of children in institutions. For example, almost all institutions have now abandoned the farms which were so productive and cost effective in years past because government regulations say they can no longer utilize their available orphan pool. Even in campus maintenance, children can do little to help because of restrictive rules. In many instances, children are prohibited from using power equipment, which means they cannot mow lawns or do other chores which require use of any power equipment. Instead, hired labor has replaced the children in such area, and added significantly to operating costs. Consider that in years past, children ran the farms, the dairies, did the laundry, repaired and in some cases made some of their own clothing, built furniture for the cottages, etc. In the name of child abuse prevention, most of these things are now no longer possible. Result - the institutions must now have a higher per capita budget to operate and perhaps equally or more important, the children have lost the opportunity to learn needed lessons in the value of the work ethic - something they will need in later years.

To look back from today's perspective at orphanages of 100 years ago one may be justifiably appalled at what was regarded as acceptable care in those days. Certainly the standards of the times have changed and are constantly changing, for the most part for the better. Nevertheless in the name of improved child care much has been lost that might have been better saved.

~ 9 ~

The Cochran Era

lthough entitled *The Cochran Era* in recognition of the importance of the UMCH's most recent and current administrator, Mr. Beverly Cochran, this chapter is very much concerned with a number of major changes in philosophy and practice, changes that have occurred at the Home in the past thirty odd years during the tenure of Mr. Cochran. While he may not have originated many of these changes, he has certainly been a factor in their acceptance and adoption at the Home.

Bev Cochran, as he is familiarly known about the campus (the children also call him Daddy Warbucks after the character in the popular Broadway hit *Annie*) came to the Home in 1969. A native of Augusta, Georgia, Cochran went to Georgia Tech on a football scholarship, and then transferred to Wofford College in Spartanburg, South Carolina for his last two years. He also attended the Universities of North Carolina and South Carolina and has

Administrator Beverly Cochran, 1969-Present

degrees in Psychology and Business Administration. He began working with children in Columbia, South Carolina, as a probation officer for the Juvenile Court of that state. He then spent three years as a social worker with the South Carolina Industrial School for Boys before accepting the position as Director of Social Services at Epworth Children's Home, the Methodist children's home for the South Carolina Conference.

He returned to Georgia in 1966 as administrator of the Plantation Manor Children's Home (now the Elks Aidmore Home) in Conyers, Georgia. In 1969 he joined the Decatur UMCH as administrator, a position he has now held for over 30 years. In years past it seems that the most important criterion for the administrator position was that the individual be an ordained Methodist minister; if he also had training and/or ability in child and institutional management that was fine but it was a lesser concern. With the appointment of Cochran, training and experience in institutional management was the first concern and the need for an ordained Methodist minister was considered unessential. The shift in qualification requirements was a good one. Thanks to his considerable experience, his natural ability, and his unquestioned devotion to the children, he has served the Home effectively through good times and bad and has guided it through periods of significant and potentially disastrous change. He has been a bulwark of stability, able to minimize the traumatic impact of changes, which some observers have felt were inappropriate while others were equally convinced of their appropriateness. Some of the changes are described in the previous chapter (*Changing Concepts*) and elsewhere in this book.

The UMCH has undergone major changes during the Cochran administration. Major administrative changes in job function and title have occurred. The position of Superintendent has been replaced by the Administrator. The Agent position has been replaced and changed to Director of Public Relations and Development. This latter position is now clearly more than fundraiser; it also includes other responsibilities.

Perhaps the most important single change that has occurred during the Cochran administration has been the change in

92

emphasis from caring only for the individual child to caring now, not only for the child, but also for his/her environment, i.e., the family. This expansion of responsibility on the part of the UMCH is evident in the offices, activities, and budgetary allotments that have evolved in recent years. We now have special programs for counseling parents, providing emergency support for financially or otherwise stressed families, etc.

Services now provided by the Home can be divided into two major categories based on who is served. These are: the **Placement Services**, and the **Family Preservation Services**.

The **Placement Services,** the better known of the two are classically associated with childcare facilities. These services include -
1. Foster Family Care - which provides a residence and services for children of any age who are in need of care by one of the foster care families serving the Home.
2. Group Residential Care - the classical institutional care for many years (at the campus at 500 Columbia Drive); provides a residence and services for children six years of age and older, many of whom may have more serious problems than foster care children.
3. Emergency Family Housing - actually a combination of Placement Services and Family Preservation Services, provides temporary housing and other support on the Campus for entire families during periods of severe family crisis, economic or otherwise.

Family Preservation Services encompass a number of support activities including -
1. Family Counseling - to help improve family relationships and help avoid the need for out placing of the children.
2. Parenting Skill Classes - training courses for parents and others to enhance relationships with their children in order to help many retain custody of their child rather than lose him/her to the placement system.

3. Emergency Financial Aid - to help families cope with financial crises and avoid child placement simply for economic reasons.
4. After Care - available to custodian after a child is returned to his/her family after spending time in the placement system.
5. Information and Referral - to help families and children locate other support groups (agencies) that offer additional services.

Because of the numerous changes that were occurring in the UMCH program in the 1960s, the Board of Trustees felt a need to review and codify recommendations that reflected the new policy goals. In 1970 the trustees created a Long Range Planning Committee that re-evaluated the status of the Home and made a number of recommendations for changes in operational policies. Some of these changes were implemented immediately, while others were to be implemented as practical. In brief, these recommended changes included:

1. The UMCH-Decatur expand its service beyond the then current residential program to include foster family care, family counseling, emergency family care, consultation and referral service for families in need, support for higher education for older children, and establishment of regional service offices.
2. The UMCH campus be retained at its present site and buildings modified as necessary to function effectively with developing needs.
3. A limit of 60 resident children be established, with the children housed in groups of no more than ten per residence cottage.
4. Several cottages be remodeled to accommodate both boys and girls.
5. All resident cottages be remodeled to include food preparation and serving within each cottage.
6. A foster home program be established to complement the residential housing program.

7. A second group home be established in a major community other than Atlanta (but within the North Georgia Conference)

8. The name of the Agency be changed to reflect its expanded role as a multi-service institution and no longer simply a "children's home."

9. The central dining facility in Hawkins Building be maintained to serve for special events as determined by the Administrator.

10. A portion of the land at the rear of the campus to be sold and funds used for future building projects.

11. Special education service be made available for those children who require more than public schools can provide.

12. Permit children of various religious faiths to participate in alternate church programs.

13. Strive to upgrade the UMCH -Decatur rating given by the Department of Family and Children's Services (DFACS).

14. Consider establishment of a day care facility utilizing locally available expertise.

15. Evaluate the feasibility of creating an emergency placement facility.

16. If an emergency placement facility is agreed upon, then use outside professional guidance in developing the program.

17. Employ a professional public relations firm to assist in presenting the Home's present and proposed programs to the public.

18. This study committee be re-designated as a long range planning committee and charged with the responsibility of annually reviewing status of recommendation implementation.

This rather lengthy list of proposed actions recommended by the Long Range Planning Committee of the Board of Trustees serves to point the directions in which the Home would and has moved. With few exceptions the recommendations promulgated by the Long Range Planning Committee have been implemented or at least work is ongoing towards their implementation. Exceptions are:

Item 7 - establishment of a second group home in the North Georgia Conference area. It was decided that most needs can be met by the present Decatur facility and unless a substantial grant be received directed specifically for this purpose, such a project is not feasible. (More recently, plans have been developed for establishment of a new group home in the Gainesville, Georgia area. Current thinking is that a facility located outside of the Atlanta area may be better utilized by rural Georgia families who are often hesitant about committing a family member to life in the "big city."

Item 8 - proposed name change to reflect expanded role. It was decided that a better understanding of the public relations impact of a name change was needed before such a change be made.

Item 11 - addition of special education program for needy children. Deferred with the thinking that this is a responsibility of the county (DeKalb), which already has an acceptable program for helping children with special needs.

Item 14 - development of a day care facility. Deferred as inappropriate and because the county now has adequate day care facilities.

Item 17 - utilize outside public relations expertise to inform public about the Home. Decided instead to develop the in-house Department of Public Relations and Development. Dr. Wilton Moulder was appointed the first head of this Department. Dr. Moulder, who retired in 1996 after 26 years of service, significantly enlarged what had been primarily a fund-raising activity to include, in addition, an active program to educate the community about the UMCH and to promote increased interaction between the community and the Home.

In spite of lengthy lists of things proposed, or done, or rejected, there is limited physical evidence of change on the campus. In 1950, the Home donated several acres of land to DeKalb County to permit construction of Forrest Hills Elementary School in the neighborhood. In 1972, the Home began renovating all cottages to provide kitchen and dining facilities (as had been tried successfully in the 1940s with Leigh cottage). All cottages were modified by 1974.

That same year, Glenn and Leigh cottages were restructured to become co-ed cottages. Glenn cottage houses young brothers and sisters plus occasionally single children. Leigh cottage became a housing unit for older boys and girls; this was later changed to an all girls cottage when it became too problematic to house older girls and boys together.

In 1979, reflecting the emerging concern for family welfare, an apartment was opened to serve as temporary emergency housing for homeless families. Later, in 1992, this apartment was shut down when the Goodwin-Wood complex of four apartments was opened. In 1998, another complex of four apartments, the Ruff-Cochran complex was opened.

In 1987-1988, the Hawkins Building (central dining facility) was renovated and joined to the new Child and Family Service Building (administration) to provide a more efficient single facility for delivery of services and goods to the Home, and to permit better coordination for the administrative and public relations activities of the Home.

Perhaps the most visible change of all was the shutting down of all farm activities in 1970. Much of that land has since been sold to developers and converted into residential neighborhoods.

More important than the visible changes have been the sociological, directional changes, which have had greater impact on the Home's operation than any physical changes. Following is an enumeration of major philosophical, sociological changes that have occurred in the past 40 years.

In early 1970, a change of admission policy was introduced permitting children of other than the Methodist faith to be allowed to attend the church of their own denomination rather than the Methodist Church.

In February, 1971, the Home signed the Civil Rights Compliance Act stating that it would not discriminate against children of any race, creed or national origin.

That same year the Home began to provide increased service to families rather than just children, by providing emergency family assistance, consultation with families, information and referral service, and eventually parent teaching classes to those who may not have known where to seek help.

In 1973, the foster care service was introduced to supplement the residential campus program and to help locate families for some of the children. This was and is in keeping with the newer policy of out placing children whenever possible.

Finally, in 1976 and 1977, the district office concept was formalized and the first district office was opened in Augusta. In 1983, a second district office was opened in Dalton, and in 1996, a third district office was opened in Rome where it serves the Rome-Carrollton District. These three district offices provide the same services for their areas as the Home does except that they do not provide the residential group care offered by the Decatur facility.

Administrator Cochran has done a remarkable job implementing all of the changes that have been dictated by the modern philosophy of caring for institutionalized children. However, there is no way he could have been successful at this without the help of a dedicated and competent staff. These people, to a man (or woman), are among the most dedicated, committed persons one could find. They work long, strenuous and stressful hours and receive limited recognition or financial compensation.
The organizational structure divides the staff into five main categories:

1. Administrative Department
2. Department of Public Relations and Development
3. Department of Community Services
4. Department of Campus Life
5. Department of Plant Operations

Following are some of the major divisions within four of the five departments and persons in supervisory positions as of year 2000. Not listed are the remainder of the staff within these divisions.

The Administrative Department includes, in addition to the Administrator (Beverly Cochran), the Director of Public Relations and Development (Richard Puckett); the Editor and Associate Director of Public Relations (Katha Morgan); the Administrative Assistant for Personnel (Jayne Irminger); and the Assistant Administrator for Finance (Reba Kimmons).

The Department of Community Services includes the Director (Steve Hubbard); Supervisor in Augusta (Russell Barrett); Supervisor in Dalton (Mike LaChapelle), and Supervisor in Rome-Carrollton (William Beaver).

The Department of Campus Life includes the Director (Jeff Amos); Activities Chief (Dan Morgan); Chaplain (Lisa Williams); Chief of Cottage Life (Shirley Ellison); Educational Services (Anne Henry); Health Services (Barbara Hill-Coatney); and Social Work Services (Terence Johnson).

The Department of Plant Operations includes the Director (Dee Strickland) and Assistant Director (Jimmy Hearn).

Girls from Williams Cottage 1989

Coming home from school 1989

Two UMCH girls and staff member
on steps of Moore Chapel 1989

~ 10 ~

UMCH Recollections

P erhaps the most informative and interesting part of a
children's home history is to be found in the recollections
of former residents. Their perspective is unique,
personal, real, and very poignant. Here are some typical
recollections of former residents who without exception describe
their days at the Home as a time of happiness and togetherness.
At a recent annual reunion of former residents, the author was
amazed to find a cohesiveness, loyalty, and camaraderie that one
would never expect to find among participants at a reunion of
regular former students, even including boarding school
students. This commonality of feeling did not seem to be
affected by at what age the child had entered the Home or how
long he or she had been a resident. Once there they seem to have
been infected with a love and appreciation for life as a resident
of the Home. And this was still apparent amongst men and
women who had left the Home over 40 or 50 years ago. As
several former residents pointed out to the author during
interviews, this may not have appeared to be such a great place
from an outsider's point of view, but from the perspective of the
resident it was always far better than what they had left to come
here.

During discussions, which the author had with individuals and
groups during the 1998 annual reunion, there was the rare
recollection of mistreatment by fellow residents or overzealous
staff but these were uncommon events and always minor. Almost
overwhelming was the universal expression of joy at seeing old
housemates and friends, and recalling events from the past

shared by others as their own unique experiences which could never be fully understood or appreciated by outsiders. It is difficult for an outsider (at least this author) to understand what it was about life in the Home that could generate such a bubbling of enthusiasm among alumnae that has persisted for so many years after leaving the Home.

One obvious bias may be introduced in this collection of resident recollections. All of the respondents were from a narrow time frame in residency (1936 to 1955), and thus do not necessarily speak accurately of home life in the earlier years or in the later years, most especially since the 1970s when a number of significant changes were taking place at the Home. For better or worse, from the author's point of view, the years encompassed by the recollections presented here probably reflect a time when life at the Home was "as good as it gets."

Here are some of the residents' recollections in their own words:

James Burch, 1936 to 1942, entered at age 12

I came to the Methodist Children's Home as an orphan at the age of 12 along with my younger brother in the early autumn of 1936. I ended my stay in 1942; those were a hard six years but were the best six years of my teenage years. I am reminded of an Oscar winning movie back then that was entitled "The Best Years of Our Lives"... those six years were truly the best years of my life.

When I arrived at the Home the Superintendent was Reverend Ralph Hawkins. He was followed by Reverend Fred Glisson from 1936 to 1939. Reverend Frank Quillian was Superintendent for one year from 1939 to 1940, and then Mr. Henry Mays from 1940 to 1944. I remember Mr. Glisson as an avid gardener, beekeeper and bird lover. I never knew if or where he kept beehives on the campus, perhaps way down in the "bottoms" - that land at the very back of the fields. He kept a garden directly across from the Hemphill Cottage, the

102

Superintendent's residence, that we called the sunken garden because it had steps leading down to a low area surrounded by high steep banks covered with flowers. Mr. Glisson was very active in visiting churches in the area to promote support for the Home; he was in my estimation, a true ambassador of good will for the Home.

I was initially assigned to the Nickerson Cottage, which housed boys from 10 to 13; I was 12 at the time. My first job was raking leaves from one end of the campus to the other. When we finished at one end we went back and started again at the beginning. This continued all winter. We also hauled coal to the cottage for heating in the winter. When spring came we cut the grass with hand mowers (no power mowers at that time). In addition to these regular chores, we also cleaned the cottage each day and did odd jobs as required.

I moved from Nickerson to Sheddon Cottage when I reached my 13th birthday. It housed boys from 13 to 15 at that time. Mr. and Mrs. Swiff Davis were houseparents at that time and served in that capacity from 1925 to 1943. Mrs. Davis had first come to the Home in 1914 under the tutelage of her uncle, Reverend J. M. Hawkins, who was Superintendent. After seven years at the Home, she returned to her home place in Banks County and married her school sweetheart, Mr. Swiff Davis, on Christmas Day, 1927. They moved back to the Home and eventually to Sheddon Cottage and Mr. Davis became supervisor of the dairy and other farm operations while Mrs. Davis supervised the older girls in the laundry. The Davises were clearly beloved by the children as well as the staff. (The author found in interviews with former residents that all spoke highly of the Davises as intelligent, fair-minded, good people.)

There were three entrances to the campus off Columbia Drive just as there are now. The first entrance that was used by most of us had a concrete entrance only. The middle entrance with two brick columns on each side was paved and led to the front of the present administration building. This stretch of concrete was ideal for skating and was so used by many children, there being few automobiles back then. The most southerly entrance was a narrow unpaved dirt road that went behind the administration building and eventually connected with the paved road from the north. There were no paved sidewalks or parking lots on the campus at that time. The dirt road beside the chapel ran behind the two cottages that housed the preteen and teenage girls and ended at the laundry and garage.

In 1936 there were six cottages, three for boys and three for girls. There was the superintendent's quarters, the Moore chapel and the Hawkins dining hall. Also there was a laundry building and the dairy barn located some distance away from the residential area. In all there were ten buildings not counting the two barns. The whole campus included about 250 acres of land with the outlying area being used for farming and pasture.

Of all the buildings on the campus none was more prominent than Moore Chapel. Built in 1906 it was a place of reverence for all the children and the faculty. Each Sunday evening we had Vespers where we met for about an hour and sang songs and listened to and participated in the teachings of Jesus and the Apostles. We were fortunate to have members of Decatur First UMC to worship with us and to conduct some of the services. Two regular participants from Decatur First that were favorites that I remember were Ann Kirby and Mildred Tilley.

The dining hall, the Hawkins Building, was a two-story structure, which included a dining room, a kitchen, and a refrigeration or milk room on the first floor and a classroom, teachers' quarters and living quarters for a maintenance worker and his wife who ran the laundry.

Just outside the dining hall was a large bell mounted on a wooden post [the bell is still there though no longer mounted on a wooden post]. It was rung to call the children to assembly and to school. The bell has an interesting history. Just after the Civil War, the bell was purchased from a Villa Rica Methodist church with the help of the prominent Asa B. Candler family and donated to the Home.

104

In 1939, the Joseph B. Whitehead school building was erected and it was far superior to the one room school above the dining hall that we had used before. Unfortunately, I never attended this new grade school that had separate classrooms for each grade.

In the spacious basement of the Whitehead Building a workshop was established under the direction of two competent carpenters who taught and supervised older boys who wanted to learn woodworking. We made all of the beds and many of the furnishings for the cottages. The highest grade taught at the Home at that time was seventh grade. After that we went to schools in town. I spent six months at the Home school and then went to Avondale Public High School. I remember at least one boy who went to Boys High School in Decatur. Some of those who finished at Avondale or Decatur went on to LaGrange College, Young Harris College, or North Georgia College in Dahlonega. In those days the Warner Hill Bible Class of St. Mark Methodist Church paid part or all of the college costs for our students. After I graduated from Avondale High School in 1942, I went on to North Georgia College.

The aforementioned Warner Hill Bible Class also was instrumental in establishing our Boy Scout troop at the Home. They furnished our uniforms, equipment, and supported many activities associated with the scout program. One of our scouts became the youngest Eagle Scout ever in the Atlanta-Decatur area at age 13. Among members of the Warner Hill Bible Study group were Mr. Frank Quillian, Superintendent of the Home for one year, 1939-1940, and Mr. Percy Plant who served as scoutmaster of our troop at the Home.

All of us were expected to work during some of our non-school hours. Boys mostly did the farm chores. If you were 12 or older and able to lift a hoe, you spent many hot afternoons plowing, planting and cultivating with the help of two stubborn old mules that hated our existence. We grew our vegetables for the Home in the fields and in the large garden just behind the Atlanta and Williams cottages.

We also worked in the dairy where we milked some 15 to 20 cows twice a day - at 5 a.m. and 5 p.m., 365 days of the year. We learned quickly to control or shackle cows so they would not turn over milk buckets. When they did, the barn cats had a field day with the spilt milk. When all the cows had been milked, we loaded the 3 or 4 ten-gallon cans of milk onto a wooden cart and hauled it uphill to the milk (refrigeration) room at the dining hall.

For some reason, I was designated to work in the laundry's boiler room with Mr. E.C. Carlisle, the Maintenance Supervisor. This was hot and difficult work. The boiler supplied steam for the laundry, heat for the dining hall and other areas, hot water for washing, and power for the laundry washer and mangle. As I recall we had to start up the boiler three to four times a week .

The older girls who worked in the laundry had an even rougher job than the boys. On hot summer days with very little ventilation in the rooms, they had to endure the heat from a red-hot pot-bellied stove used to heat their flat irons. Adjacent to the ironing room was a drying room where linens were hung on hot water-heated galvanized pipes to dry. Except for a noon lunch break, the girls had to stand all day working in this area with perspiration streaming down their faces. For all of that, they always had a smile and never complained. They were a rare breed and I salute every one of them.

Life was not all hot work. We had a swimming pool located a short distance from the well that fed cold spring water into the swimming pool and then overflowed into the lake beyond. On the hottest days we would dive off the edge into the cold water that cooled you off in a hurry.

We also had local entertainment and travel adventures. The two movie theatres in Decatur welcomed us on a given night, weekly, with no charge. Most every summer, a large number of the boys and girls got to go to Camp Glisson in Dahlonega, Georgia, for a week. One summer we all made a trip to the beach at St. Simons, Georgia, and stayed in a vacation hotel near the ocean. On another occasion some members of the scout troop were privileged to spend a week at the Bert Adams Scout Camp near Vinings, Georgia. During the Christmas Season we were always invited by various churches for parties and gift giving; Grace Methodist, Pattillo Memorial, Park Street, and First Methodist in Marietta come to mind. We were always fortunate to have such a wonderful relationship with the surrounding churches.

I am profoundly thankful and fortunate to have spent six short years here in the Methodist Children's Home as an orphan and am privileged to call it my home.

Bob Bell (and 3 brothers), entered at age 9, (1938 - 1942)

I was placed in the Home, along with my three brothers in 1938. We all stayed until 1942. Unlike many of our contemporaries, we were not placed in the Home because we had no parents. Our father had died but our mother was a loving, dedicated parent who, during those Depression years, simply could not afford to support her family given the sudden loss of the family breadwinner. She had indicated to officials that we were not to be separated, placed in foster care, or adopted out as she intended to reclaim her children as soon as she could afford it, which she did four years later. Also, more fortunate than many, we were visited every week or two by Mother who was determined to maintain the family bond in spite of the difficult circumstances.

Arriving at the Home as a nine-year-old, I was initially placed in Walton Cottage along with my younger brother; the two older brothers went to Sheddon Cottage. In Walton we lived in a large dormitory-like room and slept three to a bed. As we grew older we were moved to other cottages; I first went to Smith Cottage, and later to Sheddon Cottage.

Our Superintendent was Mr. Fred Glisson, an ordained Methodist minister; he was later followed by Mr. Frank Quillian who we called "Brother Frank." The staff persons I recall best of

107

all were Mr. and Mrs. Swiff Davis. He was in charge of the farm operation and she was housemother for Sheddon Cottage. They and their daughter shared one room in Sheddon Cottage, which must have been very crowded. He not only ran the farm operation but also served as disciplinarian for much of the Home. Mornings he would walk through Sheddon telling all to get up and get a move on. He would return about ten minutes later and woe be it to anyone who was still in bed. A child guilty of some infraction and caught, usually had to face Mr. Davis. He was a strict disciplinarian and not afraid to mete out what he considered appropriate corporal punishment.

Nevertheless he and Mrs. Davis were greatly admired and adored by the children. He was a hard worker totally dedicated to the children. His work schedule was "24-7," that is 24 hours a day, seven days a week. Years later (1999) a group of alumni erected a marker on campus as a memorial to the Davises, some indication of the affection the children had for this family.

During my years at the Home we had an elementary school right on campus (Whitehead Building) with classes up through the 6th grade; then we went to Avondale School in Decatur.

We all were assigned to work chores and I was luckier than most. While most boys had to get up and work the farm, milk the cows etc. in the early morning hours, another boy and myself were designated as "houseboys." When the others went out to do the farm chores, we stayed in the cottage and made all the beds and cleaned the cottage.

I lived at the Home during the World War II years. We were constantly warned about the potential for attack by the Germans or the Japanese and what to do in event of an attack or an air raid. My job during air raids (which of course we never had) was to stay at the campus bell and ring it if I sighted enemy aircraft. This would warn the residents to seek shelter in their assigned areas. I never knew why I got this job; perhaps because of my last name I was judged the appropriate person.

On Sundays we always got an informal sermon during mealtime from the Superintendent who sometimes talked so long that it upset the houseparents who expected us back after breakfast to do our chores. We then went to church in Decatur after which we had free time until late afternoon. At 5 p.m. we had services in the Moore Chapel, which might be conducted by different persons, usually from one of the nearby churches.

We had plenty of time for recreation. Often we went to the movies in Decatur. The movie house would let us in for free in groups of 10 or fewer.

The Home was a good place for us children. It was and is a monument to the dedication of staff that operated it. They worked long, hard hours with spare compensation and always with the welfare of the children as their main concern.

Flora Cramer, entered at age 11, (1941-1947)

My parents were farmers in central Georgia where I was born. We were a large and close family until my father died. At that time my mother was ill and not expected to live. She could not take care of us and we were scattered in different directions. I was placed in the state's custody and started on the "orphan circuit." Initially this meant foster home living. For various reasons we foster home children seldom stayed with one family for very long. By the time I was 11 I had had five sets of "parents" and over 150 "brothers and sisters." Sometimes I was the only child in a foster home and sometimes I was one among many. In some households I was dearly loved and cared for, while in others I was ridiculed and shunned. Each move meant adjusting to the new family and its ways. Each family had its own social standards, financial status, and religious convictions. What was OK in one household might be a sin in the next and vice versa. After several years of this unstable, changeable life I had almost lost my personal identity.

When I arrived on the campus of the UMCH (The Home) my whole life changed completely. First, I found living there, three of my very own brothers whose existence I had almost forgotten. I also found that my mother was still living though I had been told long ago that she had died. For me, moving to the Home was the beginning of six unforgettable years that helped erase the earlier years of instability and confusion.

Life at the Home was structured. We were assigned duties and responsibilities and had schedules to follow. If you didn't fulfil your obligations there were restrictions and punishment. If you did well there were rewards. We had the security of knowing what was expected of us and what would be the consequences of our actions - good or bad.

At the Home we functioned as a large extended family. We took care of one another if we got sick. We helped one another with school assignments, we learned to care for one another and praised and criticized one another in a fair and loving way. In short, we were a family, albeit a large one.

We never lacked for essentials. We knew we would not go hungry, that we would have clothes that fit, our own beds at night, and always - friends.

We had advantages in so many ways. We went to the movies each week, and to the circus or the opera or other special events when they were in town. Whenever an event did not "sell out" we were invited to go at no cost. Many civic organizations would invite us to their functions. I think I ate as many "peas and potatoes" dinners as most politicians.

Christmas was always an exciting and wonderful time. Each year we looked forward to riding specially chartered trolleys to Marietta for the day when the Methodist churches gave fantastic dinner parties in our honor. Oft times well meaning outsiders would want to take one or more of us into their homes for the Christmas holidays. While it was an admirable intent and the gifts were certainly appreciated, it was not really enjoyable. Our hosts did not realize that the "ordeal" of leaving our own huge family to spend Christmas with strangers was a terrible experience.

In the summer we could visit friends or family off campus for several weeks, and just before going back to school we had two weeks of camp, either up in the North Georgia mountains or on the coast.

Our grade school was on the campus but we went to high school in town. I graduated from Avondale High School in 1947 and because I was still a minor I was sent to live with a relative in Texas. In school, many of our Home children were outstanding students and were voted superlatives. Several were class valedictorians and most were in the top half of their grade.

After completing my schooling I became a land, geological and geophysical draftsman (woman) for 33 years. My brothers were in the military in World War II and later one became a police service technician, another became an architect, and a third, a textile engineer. There are many outstanding alumnae from the Home who have been at least as successful in adult life as their peers who had normal family lives.

We have a reunion of alumnae every year in Macon, Georgia, and "home children" come from all over the United States to renew friendships as though we had never parted.

Julie Spinks Mote, entered at age 5, (1942-1954)

My sister and I came to the Home in October 1942 when I was five years old and she was seven. We were first put in the infirmary to be examined by a doctor to insure that we were healthy and free of infectious diseases. After a few days in the infirmary, we were transferred to the Epworth Cottage where the youngest girls were housed. At that time there were four girls' cottages - Epworth, Walton, Williams, and Atlanta. I lived in all of them at one time or another. There were three boys' cottages -

Sheddon, Nickerson, and Smith. They were on the opposite side of the campus from the girls' cottages. In the middle of the campus between the boys' and the girls' cottages was the dining hall. In front of the dining hall was a covered stone well. It had been filled in, in the 1930s. The well was removed in 1954 during a remodeling of the dining hall and we were all sorry to see it go as it had served as a meeting spot where we played outdoor games or just "hung around." In the 1940s there were no sidewalks or paved roads on the campus.

There were 12 to 15 children in each cottage, I believe about 150 children in all during the 1950s. By the time we turned 12 years old each of us had assigned jobs to do and we rotated to different jobs every three months. Girls worked in the laundry. Each cottage sent the laundry to be washed once a week. We washed and mangled the sheets and pillowcases, starched and ironed shirts and dresses. The washer was like a huge tumbling barrel with holes in it (sometimes the boys' marbles would get stuck in the holes). We also had a wringer and a dryer. We had a room full of ironing boards, and a presser to do the boys jeans. Because of the heat, we had a large floor fan in the laundry and I remember a couple of times boys got cut fingers when they played with the fan.

The girls also worked in the dining hall. We set tables, served the food, cleaned the tables after the meals, and did the dishes - for 150 people every day. At one time I had an early morning job because of my athletic schedule (I played basketball and softball). I made toast for breakfast. Each meal was 20 loaves of bread, and butter was applied with a paintbrush. The only thing I ever learned to cook at the Home was tomato soup and grilled cheese sandwiches.

Boys also worked in the kitchen - cracking eggs, carrying milk cans from the cooler, etc. Mostly, they worked on the farm, milking the cows twice a day, feeding the chickens, and working in the fields. Some days they butchered hogs and dipped them into hot water in a big vat just outside the laundry. They would

112

sometimes throw body parts at the girls working in the laundry; this caused a lot of squealing from the girls.

I also worked in the infirmary quite a lot. We had to keep the place clean, wax and shine the floors, and bring the sick children food from the dining hall. Sometimes we would sneak around and make fudge at night. We hoarded the necessary ingredients from the kitchen until we had enough and then would make a batch for all of us to eat. I remember one night when the nurse came into the infirmary as we were making fudge and we threw it out the back door to avoid being caught. After she left we went out into the yard and recovered the fudge and ate it.

In 1950, the Leigh Cottage was opened as a residence for very young children and babies. Two of the older girls (13-18 years old) had to live in the Leigh Cottage to care for the small children. My sister and I spent three months in Leigh Cottage caring for the young children. We had seven babies from 6 months old to 3 years old. It was not a good experience as far as I was concerned and I decided then I would never have children of my own (I have since had three girls and one boy).

The campus covered about 150 acres and we had cows, pigs, horses, plowing mules, two Shetland ponies named Major Doll and Tony, and a donkey. Bob Hope, the entertainer, had given us a saddle for Major Doll and we trained him to do a few tricks. We also had a red show dog named Chow Chow. He must have lived there for 10 or 12 years. One housemother, Mrs. Staub, would send him to the veterinary clinic every summer to get trimmed and he came back looking like a lion with a big hairy mane and clean-shaven elsewhere except for his feet. Chow Chow seemed to know all the children that lived at the Home and was not too friendly when other children came around.

We ate meals in the dining hall cafeteria style. We stood in line to be served food and then ate at tables set for each cottage. At mealtime they rang the big bell outside - once to tell you to get ready, and the second time to come and eat. When everyone had gone through the food line they rang a small dinner bell and said the blessing but by then most of us had already eaten. Most of the food was grown right there on the farm. We also had good cooks; two of them had been there for over 20 years.

We didn't work all of the time. We got to go to the movies every week, and to the circus and other events when they were in town. During the summer we were allowed to swim in the public swimming pools in Decatur and around DeKalb County. We also got to go to summer camp up in the mountains and to the beach at St. Simons, Georgia. At St. Simons we stayed at Camp Marion across from the Coast Guard station and when we went swimming the Coast Guard men were our lifeguards.

We went to school in our own schoolhouse from the 1st through 6th grade and then went to school in town from 7th grade on. We were divided among several schools, Avondale, Hooper, Alexander, Scottdale, and Forrest Hills.

Brenda Reinhart, entered at age 10, (1950- 1955)
David Reinhart, entered at age 7, (1950-1955)

My brother David and I entered the Home in 1950 when he was seven and I was ten years old. Our father had been killed in an accident on Christmas Eve 1948. Shortly after that our mother became ill and we were placed in the Cedartown Home until Reverend Kerr (Superintendent of the United Methodist Children's Home in Decatur) could pick us up and take us to the UMCH Home. The day we arrived there it was after the dinner hour and we were hungry. Newly arrived children were placed in the infirmary first so that the nurse, Mrs. Brock, could make sure we weren't ill. All they had to eat in the infirmary was bread, mayonnaise, and ketchup. That's how David and I learned to eat this new kind of sandwich. As a youngster at the Home I frequently had one childhood illness or another, such as mumps and measles.

After clearing through the infirmary I was assigned to Walton Cottage. David went to Epworth Cottage. Mrs. Mosher was our

114

housemother at Walton and she was very kind. In the evenings she would sit us in a circle on the rug in the living room and read from the Nancy Drew books. At Christmas we had a Christmas tree in the cottage and we all got hard candies and other sweet treats and gifts. It felt as if we were all part of one large family celebrating the Holiday Season.

When I first went to the Home I felt different from the others because I was from the North and by definition "a Yankee." But during our time there my brother and I made many friends. I have kept in touch with some through the years, while others I may see only at the annual reunions.

Not long after arrival I moved into the Williams Cottage with the older girls. We had fun on Saturdays when we did the house cleaning and waxed and buffed the floors. While doing the household chores we would listen to the weekly 'Top Ten" list of country songs on the radio. We also worked in the laundry mangling sheets and ironing the boys' jeans (not one of my best talents for sure), all the while sweating from the steam and heat. Mr. Laws, who ran the laundry at that time, was sometimes cranky and unsmiling but I assumed it was from the heat and I liked him anyway. Sometimes there were boxes of comic books behind the laundry building that someone had donated and we were allowed to read them after our work was finished. I preferred to work in the laundry on Saturday rather than change bed linens since the iron beds gave us shocks when we put on the new linens.

We had a lot of fun at the Home. I remember that sometimes a few of the girls would sneak out from our cottage by way of the window to buy candy for all of us with money we had given them. Once, just as they were climbing out the window, the housemother came in and they had to hang by their fingers from the stone windowsill until she left and they could drop to the ground. Then they had to go to town and buy the candy and get back before it became too late at night.

Another time, we were having a pillow fight and there were feathers all over the place when Mr. Kerr (Superintendent) brought in a group of church visitors to see the cottages. I'll always treasure the memory though at the time we didn't know how much trouble we might be in. One time I was playing solitaire on the steps of Moore Chapel when Mr. Kerr came to the door with another church group. He made me put the cards away and I was sure I was going to be punished - I was not.
There was one housemother, Mrs. Ledbetter, who later became a missionary to Algeria. She would have us all sit in chairs in a circle for evening Bible reading and prayers. Each girl would take a turn giving the prayer. It reminds me of the family devotion scene in the movie Gone With The Wind, which is even today, one of my favorite movies.

There was a good lady, Miss Tillie, who used to take us to the movies each week and swimming on hot summer days. I will always remember her soft voice and smile and be grateful to her for giving us the chance to go out and enjoy a good time.

We also played "kick the can" and "jump board" in the afternoons, sometimes until dark. We used all kinds of "found" objects and our imaginations at play. We would find a piece of glass, as close to square as possible, dig a hole in the ground for it and put flowers or other objects around to make a frame and a picture. We also built playhouses among the trees, picked pecans that fell from the trees and used them to make divinity candy when our housemothers had time to help. We played "school" and "church," taking turns being teacher or preacher. We went to Vacation Bible School in the summer; during the break from classes at VBS the boys would chase the girls and try to kiss us. We learned to run very fast.

I eventually made it "up to" the Atlanta Cottage where the oldest girls lived. I wasn't quite old enough then to drink coffee, you had to be sixteen, but I felt very grown up living in the "big girls'" cottage. We occasionally went to dance recitals that seemed magical with costumes, music, and dancing that I had

116

never seen before. Shortly before I left the Home the girls began dancing lessons; I was sorry to miss that experience.

There were times we went to different churches for services and then to family homes for dinner. Some of us would sing and recite Bible verses. The boys in Epworth Cottage, where my brother lived, would often be the ones that did the reciting. The boys in Epworth did not move as they grew older as did boys in the other cottages; for some reason they stayed longer. I also believe the rules were stricter there than in the other boys' cottages. It seems as though the boys there did not have as much fun as the rest of us. The boys had to wear their Sunday best after church when they went out to play, but were told they could not get them dirty. I remember the housemother at Epworth told my brother that I was bad because I would run up and down with my friends to keep warm while waiting for the school bus in winter - and also because I turned over the porch furniture at their cottage when she wouldn't answer the door for "trick-or-treat" one Halloween.

For the past three years (1995-1998) my husband and I have attended the reunions of former UMCH children. I have enjoyed visiting with those we have seen regularly and renewing acquaintances with others I had not seen in 40 years. All of us have had sad times in our lives or we would not have been in the Home, but the time we all spent together was something special for us. We are all "family members" with one another because of the mutual experiences we shared - some good, some not so good.

Ruth Williams, entered at age 8, 1937 - 1945

I came to the Home in 1937. I was eight years old and left eight years later in 1945. I went into the Williams Cottage the first few years and then to the Atlanta Cottage. The Williams Cottage had large dormitories. Interestingly, every night when the lights went out, everybody began calling goodnight to the others (like the

Waltons on TV). A very strict woman was assigned to oversee us, not a loving
person at all. Not doing your chores exactly right could get you a slap across the face. The Atlanta Cottage, where I went later, was much more humane than the Williams had been with more freedom. The Superintendent at the beginning [of my stay at the Home] was Fred Glisson. The girls loved him very much. He was warm and kind.

My mother would visit on Sundays. The Sunday evenings at the Chapel [Moore] were so meaningful after an afternoon of homesickness.

A favorite discipline was to get up early and go to the dining room and set the tables for breakfast. The most precious black woman named Minnie did the cooking and we all loved her. She could make fudge (the best ever of course). Another favorite chore was ironing - hundreds of little dresses for the younger ones; and looking out the window watching the slaughter and skinning of pigs outside the boiler room. We girls did more squealing than the pigs. We played a lot of softball and card games - mostly <u>Rook</u>. We loved it when the Board of Trustees met and we dressed up the dining room.

Many sad and lonely times, but overall the good outweighs the bad by far. After leaving the Home, I commuted from West End to Avondale High School where I graduated. I've always been so grateful that the Home was there for us. I moved back with my mother and later met and married my husband in 1950. We raised three children that we are very proud of and we will be celebrating our 50th anniversary next March, God willing. My husband is in rehabilitation at Warm Springs, Georgia, following a stroke or I would have spent more time with this reminiscence.

We have so enjoyed the reunions, and meeting Katha [Morgan] makes me know there's got to be a lot of good at the Home now.

118

I was three years old when my mother passed away in 1943. I was an only child and was in the care of my maternal grandmother. My mother's family was considered a large family of six, poor and uneducated. My grandfather was a railroad man, an alcoholic, member of the KKK and a physical abuser. He also blamed me for my mother's death at the age of twenty-one. She married without his consent because she was pregnant. The man that I thought was my father was in the military. I never knew him because he abandoned me after my mother's death. My grandmother attempted to raise me until it was almost unbearable with the abuse she received from my grandfather. In desperation my grandmother went to the then East Point Methodist Church pastor who was very instrumental in placing me in the Home.

I entered the Home in 1946 as an only child at the age of six. I had no comprehension as to where I was or why. The only recollection I had was "WOW, look at all those kids." I was processed immediately and placed in what was called the Epworth Cottage, commonly known as the "Little Girls' Cottage." I had a very rough first year in the on campus school. It was discovered that I had very poor vision, weak ankles, and had contracted several childhood diseases. The Home always had the means to provide for normal life at the children's home. I was, at the time, somewhat of a novelty to the Home. When visitors came to tour the Home, our Superintendent, Mr. Kerr, would always say, "This is our only only child." I still did not know what he meant at that time. I didn't realize I was an only child with so many other children there with me. It was only when the children were blended into public school in 1949 that I realized I was different from the others in the world.

Yes, we were quite different from others. We had many opportunities that other "not from the Home" classmates and friends had. I still reflect back to the Home on all of the holidays. We began our round of Christmas parties on Thanksgiving weekend. Sometimes we would attend as many as three parties a day. We had a very caring housemother in Walton Cottage, Mrs. Castlelyn, who made each of the girls two taffeta dresses to wear to the parties. You can imagine what it was like in each cottage if each child had three or four packages, how the tree would look and how excited we all were. As I reflect back, as an adult now, yes, we were very privileged. We had outside friends that wanted to live on campus with us because we got to do more than they were allowed to do.

As we grew older, all of us were taught the value of an education and encouraged to do well in school. We were encouraged to participate in extracurricular activities. I was a member of the high school band for three years and played basketball also. There were not many disciplinary problems at the Home because we knew what was expected of us. Things were pretty normal for me growing up, even to the point of my adventure running away from the Home to join the circus. I was quite an entertainer and felt that the circus could use my talents as an acrobatic act. I was also known to sing a few songs in class for everyone. Often when I attend high school reunions or the UMCH reunions, people ask me if I can still remove my eyeglasses with my feet or they remember me singing the song "Trees." No, I can't do either of those things now.

Some of my fond memories of the Home are the times we went on vacations each summer to St. Simons, Georgia, and to the mountains in North Georgia, a week at each location, and the many times we traveled, singing all the way, to different churches to sing and beg for money as we used to call it. People always seemed to enjoy our songs. During the summer we would enjoy the benefits of raising our own watermelons by having what we called "watermelon cuttings" on Sunday evenings.

We were always up to date on the latest medical needs. As a child I was very envious of Johnny Sue Smith's braces on her teeth. She was the first one to get them. Dupont Hancock and I spent many Christmases in the infirmary with Mrs. Brock, our nurse. Finally, she put us in the same room one year so we could celebrate and recover together.

120

We were also taught good work ethics. Each child had certain responsibilities   assigned to them. The girls worked in the laundry, in the dining hall, and helped with the smaller children's cottages. Our jobs were rotated every three months. The boys were assigned the milking chores and farming duties. As far as food was concerned, the Home was pretty self-sufficient. We had vegetables, cows, pigs, chickens, fruit and nut trees. We ate very well.

I was raised, twelve years of my life, at the Methodist Children's Home. There are so many times that I reflect back on those years and thank God that I was raised there. I bear no hard feelings toward anyone for placing me there. It was the best thing that could have happened to me at that time. Being raised at the Home gave me a religious upbringing, taught me to be a survivor, afforded me numerous brothers and sisters, and many childhood memories.

Barbara Andrew, was never a resident, but raised next door to the Home and had some interaction with Home children; she was a teenager in the late 1940s and 1950s.

Although I grew up next to the Methodist Children's Home I had only limited interaction with the children there. We always used the Home and the Seminary as reference points when giving directions to our home. Originally our house was the first one below the children's Home and the Seminary. Later two new homes were built between us and the Home so we had to revise directions. Then Katie Kerr Drive was cut through between our property and the Home so we had to revise directions again.

Sometimes I would go to the Home grounds and skate on their sidewalk. My brothers were sometimes invited to swim at the Home. I think the boys and girls had different swimming hours. Because our house was on the opposite side of the Home property from Decatur we did not see a lot of the children as they walked to Decatur. It seemed as though the Home kept the children more or less within the confines of the campus most of the time. I do remember that on one or two occasions when our watermelons were ripe, the boys would sneak over and help themselves to one or two. My father would yell at them, but was really happy for them to have a few. An aunt who lived nearby, kept a cow and once or twice a year her helper would walk the cow through our place and over to the Home farm. Then he would bring it back home. Much later I learned that he was taking the cow to the Home farm to be bred to their bull.

From all I saw and heard, the children raised at the Home seemed to be well dressed, well mannered, and generally became successful and responsible citizens after they left the Home.

~ 11 ~

Physical Facilities (Buildings and Grounds)

The physical facilities of today's UMCH bear little resemblance to those of 50, 75, or 100 years ago. In keeping with the changing role of the Home, especially its growth through the years, the cessation of farming, the varying size of the resident population, the changing needs of the institution, and the encroachment of surrounding home developments, numerous modifications have occurred.

A former resident from the turn of the century visiting today might not recognize much of what he would find. Among the changes are a large two-story central office and administration building with dining and kitchen facilities, and many new cottages and service buildings. They are architecturally diverse, the newest of brick and similar architectural style, the older ones still of granite and wood and varying design. The two barns are still standing, but vacant and in poor repair; there are no livestock areas or farm land, but an old abandoned wagon for hauling milk cans from the barns to the refrigeration room lies in decay among the weeds. The central laundry, once bustling with hisses of steam clouds from the laundry equipment, is now a maintenance building. There's a large attractive gymnasium with adjacent swimming pool and soccer fields in place of the agricultural fields, whose groves of fruit trees and nuts are gone. Of the water tower, only its concrete foundations remain between the Williams and Atlanta cottages; and last but not least, the well, which served as a meeting place for the children, is gone. These changes and many more might confound the visitor from the past.

Some features the returning visitor *would* recognize. Most important and most recognizable are the Moore Chapel - unchanged, at least on the outside, since its erection in 1906 (if one can discount modern air conditioning equipment down one side); the old bell in the yard that was used to call the children to meals, though not mounted as it had been during its functional years; the Jesse Boring headstone; the marble stone engraved with "Feed My Lambs - 1895," still visible though it lies partially covered by weeds; the pond in the back - not much changed from earlier times; the three entrance ways, still present though the main gate no longer is marked by brick pillars; and the walkway to the main building, now interrupted by an oval garden bed. Former residents would certainly make note of other changes - good or bad as they see them - but changes without doubt.

All seven of the existing residential cottages now have kitchens and eating facilities. The old main dining area, which once fed everyone in the Hawkins building, is used for special banquets for the residents and also for feeding visitors on special occasions. Several former cottages for children have now become homes for staff personnel. A new maintenance building was completed in 1998, and as noted earlier, several cottages now house different age/sex groups of children than in earlier years.

A number of buildings, which at one time housed children, are no longer in existence. The original farm house on the property when it was first acquired, the Epworth Cottage, funded by the Epworth League and dedicated in 1889, and the Baby Cottage, dedicated that same year, have all disappeared. The original Williams Cottage has been replaced by a new cottage of the same name. The early Boys' Cottage, known unofficially as the Sam Jones Building (because of his role in securing funds for its erection) is gone, as is the Fannie Dean Hall, which contained the dining room, kitchen, and administrative offices and was completely destroyed by fire on June 3rd, 1918. These are only some of the buildings that have disappeared over time. Several were lost to fire, while others disappeared for reasons that became as lost as the buildings themselves.

An interesting side note: The Shedden Cottage, named for Mr. R. F. Shedden, its major benefactor, and originally constructed as a home for crippled children, has somehow had a change of name to the Sheddon Cottage, presumably due to some long ago typing error, or at least that is the explanation most commonly offered.

New asphalt roads have replaced older dirt roads. Utilities have been modernized and/or replaced. Some playground equipment remains and is used by the children in good weather, e.g., swing sets, etc.

Another notable change has been the addition in the 1990s of four apartment duplexes to provide temporary housing for families with emergency needs.

The current facility is well maintained, grounds are neatly kept and buildings are for the most part well maintained. There seems a continual flurry of activity to refurbish any building that begins to deteriorate. Early in 1999, the Glenn Cottage was renovated, and in late 1999, the Leigh Cottage underwent renovation. More recently work has been done on the Whitehead Building with an eye towards keeping it in functional repair until a firm decision is made as to what will be its future.

Discounting the first three years in Norcross, the present Home began with the purchase of 247.5 acres at the Decatur location. Later in the year another 2.5 contiguous acres were added. Parcels of land were acquired or disposed of through the years. The cessation of farming in 1970 resulted in much of the land at the "back" of the property becoming surplus and being sold off to developers. Today there are only 99 acres left. There are approximately 30 buildings on the campus depending on how you count them: seven children's cottages, two independent living cottages, four emergency family housing duplexes, seven staff houses, and ten offices/miscellaneous buildings. See table on next page for a summary.

Building History and Status

Note: If "Current Use" column is empty, then "Current Use" is same as "Original Use."

Date of Construction	Building Name	Original Use	Current Use
1903	Hemphill Cottage	Superintendent's residence	Staff residence
1906	Moore Chapel	Campus Chapel	
1906	Atlanta Cottage	Girl's Dormitory	Auxiliary Flea Market and storage
1911	Sheddon Cottage	Residence for crippled children	Staff residence
1912	Nickerson Cottage	Boys dormitory	Staff residence
1906	Maintenance Bldg.	Central laundry	Plant operations and storage
1919	Hawkins Bldg.	Dining room and school rooms (pre-alteration)	Dining room and offices
1939	Whitehead Bldg.	School building	Auxiliary Flea market and storage
1942	Medical Building	Campus infirmary	
1942	Smith Cottage	Boys dormitory	Independent living for older girls
1948	Leigh Cottage	Small boys and girls dormitory	Older semi-independent girls dormitory
1948	Edwards Cottage	Older boys dorm & independent living	
1955	Glenn Cottage	Coed dormitory for younger siblings	
1960	Gymnasium	Sports activities	
1961	Greene Cottage	Superintendent's home	Staff housing
1965	Sam Bell Cottage	Middle girls dormitory	

Date of Construction	Building Name	Original Use	Current Use
1965	Kerr Cottage	Middle boys dormitory	
1966	Williams Cottage	Older girls dormitory	Older girls Dormitory (new Building)
1968	Hyatt Cottage	Boys Dormitory	
1968	Trustee Cottage	Older boys dorm & semi-independent living	
Unknown	Isom Cottage	Staff residence	
1970	800 & 808 Columbia Drive (unnamed)	Staff residences	
1987	Administration Bldg.	Addition to Hawkins Building; provides offices for Child and Family Services.	
1992	Goodwin Bldg.	Emergency Housing for homeless families (duplex)	
1992	Wood Bldg.	Emergency Housing for homeless families (duplex)	
1998	Cochran Bldg.	Emergency Housing for homeless families (duplex)	
1998	Ruff Bldg.	Emergency Housing for homeless families (duplex)	

Original Home in Norcross, a converted farmhouse. 1872, now gone

Sam Jones House, a girls' cottage. Now gone

Epworth League Cottage, former residence.
Now gone

Baby Cottage, where youngest children were initially housed. Now gone

Three in a row: Walton Cottage, Original Williams Cottage (now replaced), Atlanta Cottage.
All once residences

Moore Chapel

Administration/Hawkins Building
Offices and dining hall

Glenn Cottage, residence

Health Center

Kerr, Hyatt, and Trustees Cottages. Residences

Joseph P. Whitehead Building,
once schoolhouse and residence cottage.
Now storage and flea market building

Atlanta Cottage, once residence cottage.
Now storage and flea market building

Leigh Cottage, residence

Hemphill Cottage, now a staff residence

Nickerson Cottage, now a staff residence

Sheddon Cottage, now a staff residence

New Williams Cottage

Plant Operations Building

Ruff and Cochran Duplexes
Short term housing for families in need

Aerial view of UMCH Campus   About 1984

~ 12 ~

The Auxiliary

The UMCH Auxiliary has been an integral part of the Children's Home since its establishment in 1940. In January of that year several Atlanta area Methodist Churches were invited to establish an auxiliary group, which would assist the UMCH in any way appropriate, but particularly in the area of fund raising. The first meeting was convened on January 17, 1940 in the home of Mrs. Roland Redford of Atlanta. Mrs. Frank Quillian, wife of the then superintendent, spoke to the attendees of the needs of the children's home which might be addressed by the auxiliary and plans were formulated to enlist the help of Methodists throughout the Atlanta area. A slate of officers was elected which included:

President - Mrs. Roland Redford, St. Marks UMC

Vice President - Mrs. E. C. Houston, Glenn Memorial UMC

Recording Secretary - Mrs. J. H. Williams, Decatur First UMC

Corresponding Secretary - Mrs. H. H. McPherson,
                                                    Peachtree Road UMC

Treasurer - Mrs. W. N. Pendleton, Druid Hills UMC

Publicity - Mrs. J. R. Gramling, Collins Memorial UMC

At the second meeting, held at the Children's Home on February 21st of that same year, a set of bylaws was presented and approved. The objectives of the Auxiliary were defined and remain still, twofold, 1) to educate the members of the Auxiliary and the supporting church congregations as to what the Children's Home does and how it ministers to the needs of the children, and 2) to raise funds for the benefit of the children. Monthly meetings were scheduled to keep members current and to discuss relevant old and new business and to plan future projects. In addition it was agreed that the Auxiliary officers would meet weekly to review activities and plan future projects. The monthly meetings of the Auxiliary as a whole, and the weekly meetings of officers were (and are now) held at the Children's Home. Auxiliary members who attend the monthly meetings are expected to return to their individual congregations prepared to disseminate the information received at the Auxiliary meeting.

Initially, the fund raising was a rather modest activity. In 1940 a total of $212.65 was raised by the Auxiliary and donated to pay for heating of the Home. In 1942 the Auxiliary collected and donated $261.92 in cash and $470 in goods for the Home. Today the Auxiliary conducts a biennial flea market and bake sale to raise money. Through this and from donations that may be received from other sources the Auxiliary has increased its support for the Children's Home many-fold. From the flea market and bake sales alone, in 1998 the Auxiliary was able to contribute over $40,000. Other sources of income include the sandwich shop which opens in conjunction with the flea market-bake sale activity, membership dues - currently $3.00/year, and individual donations made by persons or organizations to the Auxiliary.

Among notable purchases for the Home by the Auxiliary have been several vehicles, the first a used car purchased in 1983 for use on the campus to teach the children how to drive, a necessity not a luxury on the campus. Subsequently several vans have been purchased and allocated to different cottages where they are used to transport the children about the city as appropriate, *i.e.* to sporting events, social outings etc. As of 1999 vehicles have been purchased with auxiliary donations for every cottage on the campus as well as trucks for the Maintenance Department and other activities on the campus.

The Auxiliary has purchased, among other items, home furnishings for the cottages, dining hall equipment, school supplies, and other items as needed. Also, it has provided travel funds for children to attend special events or visit family on special occasions. One seldom-recognized gift from the Auxiliary is the annual subscription to magazines and newspapers for the children. A major donation in 1997-1998 was over $36,000.00 towards completion of the new Cochran-Ruff emergency housing duplexes. An additional $5,000.00 was provided to purchase linens, furnishings and appliances for these residences.

In 1989 the Auxiliary created an Auxiliary Endowment Fund to be supported by a tithe from the monies made at the flea market and bake sale events. Interest income earned from the Endowment Fund principal is donated to the UMCH operating budget to help defray regular operating costs; this is in addition to monies used for the continuing purchase of specific items for the children's direct benefit. As of August 1998 the Endowment Fund had grown to $122,546.00.

For most of its existence the Auxiliary has been a project of the Methodist women. In recent years however, men and members of other denominations have begun to play a role in Auxiliary activities. Three men have been members of, and significantly involved in the operation of the Auxiliary for a number of years. They are Thomas McCollum (husband of recent Auxiliary president Geneva McCollom), Thomas Weyandt, and Bill Simpson. These men have served as treasurer, assistant treasurer and recording secretary, respectively. Also, in recent years there has been some increase in participation by retired husbands in flea market activities. Particularly in the collecting, repairing, and arranging of furniture and other heavy items the men have become a useful part of the Auxiliary.

PAST AUXILIARY PRESIDENTS

Mrs. R. A. Radford
Mrs. L. A. Williams
Mrs. Rembert Green
Mrs. Paul Robertson
Mrs. Charles Strong Jr.
Mrs. Bennet Hutchinson
Mrs. F. N. Suddath
Mrs. Vivian McDowell
Mrs. N. A. Pitman
Mrs. J. D. Blair
Mrs. L. J. McGee
Mrs. C. H. Bray
Mrs. Walter Garrard
Mrs. Virgil Crane
Mrs. Charles Taylor

Mrs. Don Boyer
Mrs. George Head Jr.
Mrs. William H. Shealy
Mrs. Jack A. Wolff
Mrs. George (Jean) Head Jr.
Mrs. Thomas E. Howell
Mrs. Prentice (Dot) Palmer
Mrs. Edward (Sonya) Craig
Mrs. Ansel (Fay) Greenway
Ms. Jo Sills
Mrs. Harold (Mary) Taylor
Mrs. H. S. (Betty) Parsons
Mrs. Mary Moore
Mrs. George (Jean) Head Jr.
Miss Mary Gresham

Mrs. William W. (Joyce) Turrentine Jr.
Mrs. O. W. Day
Mrs. Thomas (Geneva) McCollum

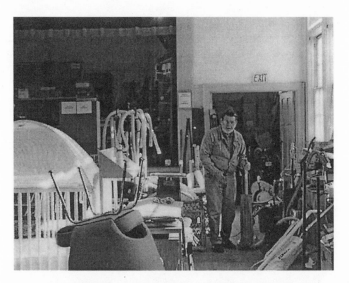

*Preparing for semi-annual auxiliary flea market
Volunteer Perry Rogers sorting items*

*Preparing for October 1998 flea market sale
Volunteers Katherine Rogers, Geneva McCollum, and
Marilyn McBroom pricing items*

~ 13 ~

The Future

As noted in Chapter 8 *Changing Concepts* and Chapter 9 *The Cochran Era,* the UMCH-Decatur and other similar institutions have had to deal with many changes in the past 4-5 decades, especially in societal needs, in operational philosophy, in governmental interrelationships, and in financial support. These multiple factors have merged into a set of policy recommendations that for the most part has been directed at removing the child from institutional housing and returning the child to his/her biological parents or placing the child in foster care, and in either case doing it as rapidly as possible. Since the 1960s, and in some cases earlier, this has become generally accepted philosophy in child care programs across the country.

However there has developed in recent years a growing dissatisfaction with this policy of downplaying the use of institutions for long term housing, and instead vigorously promoting the rapid outplacement of children either back to biological parents or to foster homes. In 1994 and 1995 the issue of long term institutional care versus rapid outplacement was a major topic of discussion among those concerned with such matters. No clear cut recommendations were developed. In 1997 a major symposium was held in Newport, California to address the topic of reforms for the various child welfare systems. Again, no consensus could be agreed upon. Child care agencies are now faced with uncertainties as to what is the best approach to serving their charges. Should they continue on the present course of outplacing as rapidly as possible, revert to the older institutionalization, or try some new and novel approach?

Increasingly recommendations are appearing suggesting that outplacing is fine - in all its variations - if <u>adequate</u> evaluation of the child-family relationship is conducted beforehand. That is, someone, be it sociologists, psychologists, or whomever must predetermine that there is a "good match", *i.e.* a high probability of success   for development of a good child-family relationship before the child is outplaced.

The newest thinking seems to be a modification and melding of the outplacing concept and the older institutionalization system. The prime motivational influence behind the newest thinking on child care management has been the influence of one Richard McKenzie. A professor at the Graduate School of Management, University of California/Irvine, McKenzie has the unimpeachable credentials of having been raised in an orphanage himself and knowing first hand the facts of life about institutional living. He has published at least two books relating to orphanages and their role in modern civilization, and in addition has published over twenty books in his chosen field of economics, particularly on the role of government as a funding source for non-governmental institutions. Today McKenzie is the outspoken guru for change in institutional child care in the United States. To attempt to summarize McKenzie's philosophy on child care would be unfair to him and to the reader. I would strongly urge anyone interested in the current and future status of child care institutions to read both his autobiography of his life in an orphanage (*The Home*) and his more technical compilation of papers by 15 recognized authorities on child care (*Rethinking Orphanages for the 21st Century*) which discusses various aspects, the pros and cons, of institutional living and other options. This latter publication is the result of a symposium held in California in June 1997 on the search for reforms needed in child care management in the United States.

McKenzie and the other authors who contributed to this latter publication spend a great deal of time explaining how we got where we are today in child care - the good and the bad- and then

146

offer solutions to the problems of today. Here is a "bullet-type" summary of the most salient points which they report:

1. The nature of today's child is different from the orphan of 50-100 years ago. Today's child is likely to have one or both parents living but to come from a dysfunctional home, may well have been abused at home, is likely to be unwanted by the natural parent(s) either for economic or other reasons, and is very likely to have moderate to severe psychological problems as a result of early mistreatment.

2. Government and sociologist advisors have decided that returning the child as soon as possible to biological parents is the most desirable course of action if at all possible. Placing the child in foster care with a family member is second choice and placing the child in foster care with an unrelated foster parent is next. These same "authorities" feel that institutionalizing the child (as in an "orphanage") is the least desirable and to be avoided if at all possible.

3. Popular thinking reflecting the evils of institutional housing is for the most part overstated and incorrect. In the past, institutional life has been a positive experience for the vast majority of children who came to the institutions from unsatisfactory home environments.

4. They conclude that: given the knowledge gained from the past experiences with Home life and given our greater understanding of child rearing outside of the home, the classic institutions are probably a far more desirable choice for many children than is generally accepted today.

5. As proof of their contentions regarding the positive value of institutional living, several of the authors make comparisons between subsequent success in life by "Home children" versus children raised in a classic family environment. The "Home children" come out very well in the comparison.

147

6. An alternative solution to modern child care may be to continue using the outplacement approach so popular today, but to modify it to the extent that greater care be spent in determining the compatibility between child and biological or foster parents prior to committing the child into that home. The institution should remain an acceptable option should outplacement not be appropriate.

To really get an understanding of the thinking of this panel of experts, one must carefully pore through the collection of papers compiled by McKenzie. Whether one agrees with all or parts of their conclusions, there is little doubt that this represents the thinking of a number of experts on the subject.

In a separate document on the same subject Professor McKenzie identifies three policy changes, which he feels, are needed to make institutional homes effective options for today's children. He suggests:

1. Lessen the regulatory burden on child-care institutions.
2. Expand work opportunities in child-care institutions (for children).
3. Convert public child-welfare funds to block grants.

On the specific issue of foster care management McKenzie offers a 12 point set of recommendations:

1. Elevate the importance of "permanence" in the development of child-welfare policies. [That is, emphasize the importance of providing the child with a lasting home, as in an institution rather than multiple short term homes as often occurs under the foster care system.]
2. Narrow the range of cases in which "reasonable efforts" must be made to reunite children with their abusive and negligent parents.
3. Assign the initial investigation of cases of extraordinary abuse and neglect to the police and the criminal justice system.

4. Establish a rebuttable presumption of unfitness in the child welfare law.
5. Shorten the timetable for the initial hearings on the termination of parental rights.
6. Speed up the notification of judicial authorities of cases of parental rights termination.
7. Establish guidelines for the permanent placement of children.
8. Place responsibility for rehabilitation on parents.
9. Make what is best for the children the central issue in cases of termination of parental rights.
10. Require concurrent case planning for both family reunification and termination of parental rights.
11. Evaluate parent's fitness to be parents at the start of child abuse and neglect cases.
12. Use public funds to encourage child care innovations.

There is clearly a growing dissatisfaction with current child care policies and the controversial issues are well identified by McKenzie and the symposium presenters at the aforementioned symposium held in June 1998 in California. Only time will tell if the McKenzie recommendations are viable or if some other approach is indicated.

Perhaps more self-examination of child care agencies is needed to sort out the good and bad policies that have been tried in the past. More collective analyses such as the one reported by McKenzie may be indicated. Hopefully a clear concise set of recommendations may evolve in the near future.

BIBLIOGRAPHY

Annual Reports of the North Georgia Conference of the United Methodist Church; United Methodist Center, 159 Ralph McGill Blvd. NE; Atlanta, Ga. 30308; 1871-1989.

Boring, Hugh. *The Boring Family History*; Author's personal publication; Wichita, KS, 1991. 461 pp.

Coleman, Kenneth A. *A History of Georgia, 2nd Ed.;* Univ. of Georgia Press, Athens, GA.; 1991. 461 pp.

Flanigan, J.C. *History of Gwinnett County, Georgia, 1818 - 1943*, Vol. 1; Gwinnett County Historical Society Inc.; P.O. Box 261, Lawrenceville, GA.; 1943. 502 pp.

Hinson, Deann P. *A History of Bethesda United Methodist Church* , Lawrenceville, GA.; Brentwood Christian Press, Columbus, GA.; 1986. 96 pp.

Holt, Marilyn I. *The Orphan Trains, Placing Out In America*; Univ. of Nebraska Press, Lincoln, NE.; 1992. 248 pp.

Jones, Mrs. Sam P. *The Life and Sayings of Sam P. Jones;* Christian Book Gallery, St. John, IN; 1907. 464 pp.

Maxwell, Mrs. Alva G. *Story of the Methodist Children's Home, Decatur, Georgia;* Administrator, United Methodist Children's Home, 500 Columbia Dr., Decatur, GA.; 1938. 30 pp.

McKenzie, Richard B. *The Home - A Memoir of Growing Up In An Orphanage*; Basic Books, Div. Of Harper Collins, New York, NY; 1996. 228 pp.

McKenzie, Richard B. *Rethinking Orphanages for the 21st Century*; Sage Publications, Thousand Oaks, CA.; 1999. 327 pp.

McKenzie, Richard B. *Rethinking Orphanages for the 21st Century*; Center of the American Experience; 12 South 6th St., Minneapolis, MN.; 1997. 24 pp.

Price, Vivian. *History of DeKalb County, Georgia 1882 - 1900*; Wolfe Publishing Co. Fernandina Beach, FL. 32035; 1997. 518 pp.

Suddeth, R.E., Osterholt, I.L., and Hutcheson, G.L. *Empire Builders of Georgia, 3rd Ed.*; The Steck Co., Austin, TX.; 1962. 559 pp.

APPENDIX A

The charter granted by the state of Georgia on November 21, 1871 to the Methodist Episcopal Church, South, for the establishment of an orphans' home to be conducted under the auspices of the North Georgia Conference.

STATE OF GEORGIA,
FULTON COUNTY.

OCTOBER TERM, 1871

TO THE SUPERIOR COURT OF SAID COUNTY.

The petition of Jesse Boring, Walter R. Branham, Habersham J. Adams, Lewis J. Davies, Weyman H. Potter, Clement A. Evans, John L. Hopkins, Thomas M. Merriwether, Charles H. Johnson, Hiram P. Bell, George N. Lester, and another, sheweth that they have been appointed Trustees of an Orphans' Home to be established by and conducted under the auspices of the North Georgia Conference of the Methodist Episcopal Church, South. That the objects of their appointment and association are to establish within the bounds of said Conference a Home for Orphans, into which the indigent Orphans of said Church and Congregations, and others when practicable shall be received and cared for, in all respects, as in intelligent Christian families; and when such Orphans shall be as thoroughly educated as practicable, trained to business and habits of industry, and useful pursuits, and, as far as possible, qualified to become useful members of Society. That their place of business and field of operations are the bounds of the Conference aforesaid, which includes the City of Atlanta, and said County, and covers that portion of said State lying north of a line running east and west (beginning at the Chattahoochee River at Pine Mountain) to Flint River, thence, down Flint River to the south line of Upson County; thence along the south line of Monroe County to the City of Macon; and (leaving Macon South) thence, along the south lines of Jones, Baldwin, Hancock, Warren, and Richmond Counties to the Savannah River. That their corporate name is "The Orphans Home of the N. G. Conference." That being a purely charitable association, they have no capital, except such contributions and donations as may be made and given by the Charitable and benevolent for the purpose and objects aforesaid, and that, therefore, there is no capital paid in. That they desire to be vested with the right and power to locate said Home at such point in the bounds of said Conference as they may deem most eligible, and to change such location when, in their judgment, the good of said Home requires the change; to receive by gift, donation purchase, or contribution any and all money and property, real or personal, necessary and proper for establishing said Orphans' Home, and conducting the same for the objects and purpose hereinbefore specified; and to hold such money and property in trust for the Methodist Episcopal Church, South, for the purposes aforesaid, and, when proper, to sell or otherwise dispose of the same or any part thereof; that they desire that they and their successors in office may be incorporated by the name of "The Orphans' Home of the N. G. Conference," and for the purposes aforesaid for, and during the term of twenty years, with the privilege of renewal, and with the right to have and use a common seal, and the same to alter at pleasure; to appoint a superintendent, matrons, teachers and such other officers and subordinates of the institution as they may deem necessary and proper for conducting and managing the same, to carry on such farming operations and other business pursuits in connection with said Home, as in their judgment, will promote the objects and compass the end of said association; and to pass such by laws, rules and regulations (not in conflict with the Constitution and laws of this State, or of the United States) as they may think necessary and proper for the management of the affairs and business of said Institution.

Wherefore, they pray the Court to pass an order granting the incorporation as sought for.

This Oct. 21st, 1871.

LESTER & THOMSON
Petitioner's Atty.

APPENDIX B

The United Methodist Children's Home

BY-LAWS

ARTICLE I

<u>NAME</u>

This non-profit corporation shall be chartered under the laws of the State of Georgia, and the Charter shall be renewed and amended from time to time as occasion or law may require. The name of the corporation shall be The United Methodist Children's Home of The North Georgia Conference, Inc., hereinafter referred to in these by-laws as the Home, with the administrative office and location at 500 Columbia Drive, Decatur, Georgia. Among other names by which the corporation is known are United Methodist Home, Methodist Children's Home, Decatur Orphans Home, and Methodist Home.

ARTICLE II

The Home shall be an independent, non-profit, social welfare agency owned by the North Georgia Conference of The United Methodist Church. The Board of Trustees shall have the power to buy, sell, and in all ways to manage the property of the Home. The title to all property shall be in the name of the Home.

ARTICLE III

<u>PURPOSE</u>

The purpose of the Home shall be to provide a Christian, family-oriented children and youth multiple service program with casework services, group residential and foster family care. In carrying out this purpose there shall be no discrimination as to race, color or sex.

ARTICLE IV

PERSONS SERVED

The Home shall serve children and families who reside within the geographical boundaries of the North Georgia Conference of The United Methodist Church. Discretion shall be left to the administrator of the Home in special cases concerning children and families who reside outside the area of the North Georgia Conference but within the state of Georgia.

ARTICLE V

BOARD OF TRUSTEES

Section 1.   Purpose of Board
The Home shall be governed by a Board of Trustees, hereinafter called the Board. The Board shall exercise all the powers, duties and responsibilities of the Home. The Board may delegate, to such committees as it may create, any of its powers that it may deem judicious, keeping in mind that it has ultimate responsibility for the Home and that it must ensure proper accountability of each of its committees.

Section 2.   Membership
Membership of the Board shall consist of:
(a) Twenty-eight (28) elected members, selected because of their interest, capability and willingness to serve on this Board. One member shall be elected from each district of the North Georgia Conference. Care shall be exercised in selecting the lay members to assure consideration of both sexes and persons from all walks of life.

(b) The administrator shall give staff leadership to the Board.

(c) Ex-officio members
The resident bishop of the North Georgia Conference; the district superintendent of the district in which the Home is located; the district superintendents of the districts in which regional offices of the Home are located; the chairperson of the Board of Heal and Welfare Ministries of the North Georgia Conference; and the agency attorney(s) shall serve as ex-officio members of the Board. Ex-officio members shall be entitled to all rights and privileges of elected members of the Board.

(d) At least ten (10) members of the Board shall be Methodist ministers of the North Georgia Conference. They may be either elected or ex-officio members.

(e) Emeritus members may be named by the Board and shall be entitled to all rights and privileges of elected members.

Section 3.   Term of Office

(a) One-fourth of the elected membership of the Board shall be elected annually to serve a term of four (4) years.

(b) A member shall retire after a maximum of two (2) consecutive terms, not including any other person's unexpired term to which he or she may be elected. A retired member may be eligible for re-nomination after a leave of one (1) year.

(c) No one shall be elected to a full term after reaching seventy-two (72) years of age.

(d) The term of service of an elected member of the Board shall begin at the annual meeting following his or her confirmation by the Annual Conference and shall end at the annual meeting four (4) years later, excepting unexpired terms for which that member was elected.

Section 4.   Attendance
If a member is absent from three (3) consecutive meetings of the Board without good cause, the Board may declare his or her position vacant.

Section 5:   Duties

(a) The Board shall set up the corporate or legal existence of the Home and give it continuity.

(b) It shall select and appoint the administrator and shall delegate responsibility to the administrator for administering the Home. No official or trustee of the Board shall assume any duty or responsibility connected with the actual care of the children. The administrator shall be bonded in an amount set by the Board.

(c) It shall see that adequate funds are available for financing the Home's operations, including adequate staff, proper working conditions, salaries and facilities.

(d) It shall govern the Home by policies and plans that it determines and approves and that are formulated with the administrator and the staff.

(e) It shall account for the service of the Home and the expenditure of funds. To be accountable, it shall make provision for proper bookkeeping and auditing; it shall set and approve the budget; it shall study reports, ask questions and keep informed regarding the Home's activities and its field of service. The bookkeeper, employed by the administrator, shall be bonded in an amount set by the Board.

(f) It shall represent the Home in the community through presentation of the Home's point of view to formal and informal groups and to government bodies,

157

and by interpretation of the Home's services.

Section 6.   Meetings
(a) A minimum of two (2) board meetings shall be held annually.
(b) Called meetings of the board may be held at the request of the chairperson, or no less than six (6) members of the board. Ten (10) days written notice, stating the purpose of the called meeting, shall be mailed to all members prior to the meeting.

Section 7.   Quorum
Thirteen (13) members of the Board shall constitute a quorum.

Section 8.   Conflict of Interest
A conflict of interest exists if a trustee should vote or take part in deliberations on significant matters directly or indirectly affecting his or her income or employment or that of a member of his or her family. If a conflict of interest exists regarding a voting matter, the individual trustee has a fiduciary duty and obligation to completely disclose his or her interest in the matter and to abstain from voting.

ARTICLE VI

OFFICERS

Section 1.   Officers
The officers of the Board of the Home shall come from the Board members. The elected officers shall be chairperson, vice-chairperson, treasurer and secretary.

Section 2.   Duties
The officers shall fulfill the duties assigned by the Board.
(a) The chairperson shall be subject to the control and direction of the Board and shall

158

have general supervision of the affairs and business of the Home. The chairperson shall preside at all meetings of the Board and of the Executive Committee. The chairperson shall be a member, ex-officio, of all other committees except the Nominating Committee. He or she shall appoint all committees except when this appointment is reserved to the Board.

(b) The vice-chairperson shall act in place of the chairperson in his or her absence and shall lend assistance where required and at all possible times.

(c) The treasurer shall have general responsibility for the Home's funds and accounts, subject to the order of the Board. The treasurer shall cause proper books of accounts to be kept, which at all reasonable times shall be open to the examination of any member of the Board, and shall be rendered at such times as the chairperson or Board shall order. He or she shall make certain that the books are audited no less than annually by a certified public accountant. An assistant treasurer may be elected by the Board.

(d) The secretary shall keep accurate minutes of the meetings of the Board. An assistant secretary may be appointed to perform the duties of the secretary in his or her absence.

Section 3.   Term of Office

The term of office shall be for one (1) year. No person shall hold the same office for more than three (3) consecutive terms with exception of the treasurer who may serve more than three (3) consecutive terms in this office. The term of office shall begin at the close of the annual meeting of the Board and shall continue until the close of the next annual meeting, or until a successor has been elected.

ARTICLE VII

NOMINATIONS AND ELECTIONS

Section 1.   Nominating Committee
The Nominating Committee shall consist of the elected chairperson and four (4) other Board members elected by the Board at its first meeting following the annual meeting. This committee shall be alert for prospective board members.

Section 2.   Nomination
(a) At least two weeks prior to presenting a nomination of a new board member to the Board, the committee shall notify each member in writing the names of the persons it proposes to nominate. A brief profile describing the proposed nominee's education, church participation and experiences with social welfare and civic organizations shall also be included. At the Spring meeting, the Nominating Committee shall then officially propose a slate of nominees willing to serve as board members
(b) At the Spring meeting the Nominating Committee shall propose a slate of nominees for officers and for chairperson of the Nominating Committee.
(c) Additional nominations for any office may be made from the floor providing permission has been obtained from the person being nominated.

160

Section 3.   Elections
    (a) Election shall be either by ballot or acclamation, such choice being made by the Board.
    (b) New board members shall be subject to confirmation by the annual conference session following their election by the Board.
    (c) The Board may fill any vacancy that occurs in the interim upon recommendation of the Nominating Committee.

ARTICLE VIII

COMMITTEES AND THEIR FUNCTIONS

Section 1.   Executive Committee

The Executive Committee shall consist of the officers of the Board, the chairpersons of the standing committees and such others as are designated by the chairperson of the Board, with the approval of the Board. The chairperson of the Board shall be the chairperson of the Executive Committee. The Executive Committee shall meet upon call for the purpose of performing urgent business that cannot wait for the action of the Board, or that which cannot be handled by a functional committee of the Board. Any action of the Executive Committee shall be reported for ratification at the next meeting of the Board and, if indicated, may be reported sooner by mail. A simple majority of the members of the Executive Committee shall constitute a quorum.

161

Section 2.   Finance Committee

The Finance Committee shall be composed of
the chairperson, the vice-chairperson, the
treasurer, and at least four (4) other members of
the Board to be appointed by the chairperson of
the Board. The Finance Committee shall have
the power to buy, sell, hypothecate, exchange
and transfer real estate, personal property,
stocks, bonds and other securities and otherwise
to invest and reinvest any funds of the Home.
This committee's policies of investment,
however, shall be subject to review by the
Board. Any two members of the above
committee, or in lieu thereof, one member of the
committee and the administrator, shall be
authorized and empowered to execute on behalf
of the Home, such documents as may be
necessary to effectuate purchase, sale,
hypothecation, exchange or transfer of the above
mentioned real estate, personal and intangible
property. In all cases those signing shall note
their office and affix the corporate seal to said
document or documents. In other matters
approved by the Board, such as tax returns,
contracts, applications for tax exemption or
approval of pension plans or on various and
sundry other matters where officers are not
specifically designated to affix signatures, two
signatures as set forth above plus corporate seal
shall suffice to legally bind corporation. The
Finance Committee shall report to the Board at
regular intervals, and a complete auditor's report
on the Home's finances (including its
endowment and trust funds) shall be sent
annually to all members of the Board. The
Finance Committee shall prepare a budget in
cooperation with the administration, and the
chairperson shall present the same to the Board,

along with the committee's recommendations. Concerning the shifting of funds and addition of expenditures:

(a) The administrator shall have the power to make shifts of funds within the approved budget with approval of the Finance Committee.

(b) The Finance Committee shall make recommendations to the Board of any expenditures other than those included in the approved budget.

Section 3.   Nominating Committee

The Nominating Committee's membership and duties are defined in Article VII.

Section 4.   Personnel Practices Committee

The Personnel Practices Committee shall help to establish policies and procedures regarding salaries and annual increments, hours and working conditions, retirement and hospitalization, etc., that permit the Home to employ, train and hold a qualified staff that will foster a high productivity and quality of service. This committee shall work with the administrator in defining duties and responsibilities for all job positions and in working up necessary public and personal liability insurance.

Section 5.   Buildings and Grounds Committee

The Buildings and Grounds Committee shall have general supervision of the buildings and grounds with regard to upkeep, repairs and furnishings.

Section 6.   Services Committee

The Services Committee shall have the following functions:

(a) To provide the Board with detailed information about the Home's services that cannot be given at Board meetings, e.g., properly disguised case material presented

by staff members to illustrate aspects of the
Home's services.

(b) To allow for continuing examination of the
Home's program of services. Such includes
the quality of existing services, and possible
projected services the Home should offer in
the short and long term future.

(c) To give the administrator and appropriate
staff members an opportunity to discuss
with the Board, problems, trends and
current experience in the Home's caseload
and practice.

Section 7. Ad Hoc Committee
Ad Hoc (for this special purpose) committees
shall be appointed by the chairperson of the
Board as the need occurs. These committees
shall be formed and named and shall remain
intact until the need has been met, at which time
such committees shall dissolve themselves.

ARTICLE IX

The fiscal year for the Home shall begin on January 1 and end on
December 31.

ARTICLE X

TRUSTEES INDEMNIFICATION

The Home shall indemnify and hold harmless all trustees,
officers, and its administrator who was or is a party or is
threatened to be made a party of any threatened, pending or
completed action, suit or proceeding, whether civil, criminal,
administrative (other than an action by or in the right of the
Home) by reason of the fact that he or she is or was a trustee,
officer or administrator of the Home, or is or was serving at the
request of the Home as a trustee, officer or administrator, against
expenses (including attorney's fees), judgments, fines and

amounts paid in settlement actually and reasonably incurred by him or her in connection with such action, suit or proceeding if he or she acted in a manner he or she reasonably believed to be in or not opposed to the best interests of the Home, and with respect to any criminal action or proceeding, had no reasonable cause to believe his or her conduct was unlawful. The termination of any action, suit or proceeding by judgment, order, settlement, conviction, or upon a plea of *nolo contendere* or its equivalent, shall not, of itself, create a presumption that the person did not act in a manner which he or she reasonably believed to be in or not opposed to the best interest of the Home, and with respect to any criminal action or proceeding, had reasonably cause to believe that his or her conduct was unlawful.

ARTICLE XI

RULES OF ORDER

The rules contained in the current *Roberts Rules of Order, Revised* shall govern all meetings in all cases to which they are applicable and in which they are not inconsistent with these by-laws.

ARTICLE XII

CHANGE OF BY-LAWS

These by-laws may be altered, amended or repealed by an affirmative vote of a majority of the members present at any special or regular meeting of the Board, providing that ten (10) days written notice of the proposed action is given in the call of the meeting, and that a quorum is present.

Amended- *July 22, 1971; April 27, 1972; April 24, 1975; April 22, 1976; April 27, 1978; January 25, 1979; April 26, 1979; July 26, 1984.*

APPENDIX C

Superintendents of the Methodist Children's Home

Thomas Boring 1871-1872

W. R. Foote   1873

Joseph Carr   1874-1875

J. L. Lupo   1876-1882

P. G. Turner   1883

A. J. Gibson   1884

F. M. T. Brannon 1885-1886

T. H. Hollyman 1887-1894

S.A. Taylor   1895-1897

G. W. Griner   1898-1899

George D. Stone 1900-1902

C.A. Jamison   1903-1908

J.M. Hawkins   1909-1933

Ralph Hawkins 1933-1936

Fred Glisson   1936-1939

Frank Quillian 1940

H.B. Mays   1940-1944

B.C. Kerr   1945 -1960

F.Q. Echols   1961-1962

John C. Moore 1962-1969

B.O. Cochran   1969-present

APENDIX D

Agents of the Methodist Children's Home*

Jesse Boring	1871-1872	Fred Glisson	1937-1939
W. R. Foote	1873-1876	Frank Quillian	1940-1941
W. J. Scott	1878-1879	W. C. Crawley	1941-1942
Sam P. Jones	1880-1892	C. C. Jarrell	1943-1944
H. L. Crumley	1893-1911	B.C. Kerr	1945-1963
J. M. Hawkins	1912-1933	Wilton Moulder	1969-1995
Ralph Hawkins	1934-1936	Richard Puckett	1995-present

* Beginning in 1960 this position was given various name changes, and duties were also modified to include public relations and publicity responsibilities.

167

APPENDIX E

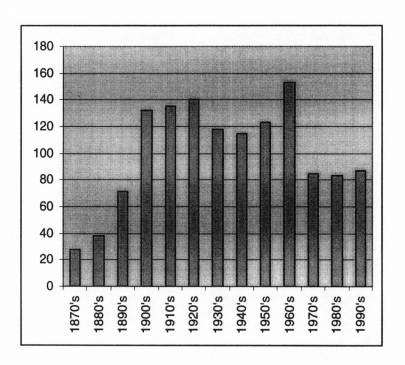

AVERAGE NUMBER OF CHILDREN IN RESIDENCE
AT THE UMCH BY 10 YEAR PERIOD

APPENDIX F

Graves of children who died at the Home and are buried in the Decatur, Georgia cemetery.

Lot 10	Lot 67	Lot 68
Comer Paine	Willie Mae Hickman	Ethel Hayes
Height Northrope	Nellie Harris	Ruby Mitchell
	Jim Harris	James Morgan
	Ola Harris	H. Rowland
	John Harris	Infant Carter
	Mattie Chambers	John McElroy
	Effie Little	Logan Wilson
	Elizabeth Reed	Grady Williams
	Mattie Rice	Wm. H. Hobbs
	Miss Paul Smallie	Janie Park
	Mary Davis	Harry Cochran
	Infant ?	John Wallace
	Andrew Hickman	Infant of C.J. Callahan
	Grady McCullough	Georgia Hayes
	Leona Rice Rollins	